THE DRAGONS KITCHEN

Published under licence by Vision Sports Publishing Limited

Welsh Rugby Union Limited
Millennium Stadium
Westgate Street
Cardiff
CF10 1NS
www.wru.co.uk

Vision Sports Publishing Ltd
19-23 High Street
Kingston upon Thames
Surrey
KT1 1LL
www.visionsp.co.uk

ISBN: 978 1 9095 3432 2

Editors: Jim Drewett, Ann Hawkins and Toby Trotman
Food stylist and recipe consultant: Angela Boggiano
Design: Neal Cobourne
Copy editor: Paul Baillie-Lane
Production: Ulrika Drewett
Food photography: Craig Robertson
Player photography: Nick Maroudias and Chris Fairweather (Huw Evans Picture Agency)
All other photography: Huw Evans Picture Agency

Printed in Slovakia by Neografia

A CIP record for this book is available from the British Library

WRU

THE
DRAGONS' KITCHEN

Celebrating the love of food, family and rugby

WELSH
RUGBY
CHARITABLE
TRUST

IN SUPPORT OF THE WELSH RUGBY CHARITABLE TRUST

feed me til.

I want no more!

CONTENTS

FOREWORD
BY HRH THE DUKE OF CAMBRIDGE

KENSINGTON PALACE

As Patron of the Welsh Rugby Charitable Trust it is both my pleasure and privilege to be closely associated with the work of this charity; the only one in Wales dedicated solely to supporting players who have suffered catastrophic injuries while playing the game they love.

There are, perhaps, few greater tragedies to befall a young player than to be at the peak of physical fitness one minute and the next to be permanently disabled. It takes a particular kind of courage and determination to come to terms with such a life-changing event, for both the player and their families.

I am pleased, through the work of the Trust, to have the opportunity to meet these players and their families during my visits to Cardiff's Millennium Stadium. To witness their continued passion for the game of rugby is truly inspirational. Both the Trust and the Welsh Rugby Union work together to ensure that this very special group of people are always welcomed within rugby's great fellowship.

The Dragons' Kitchen cookbook is a great opportunity to celebrate this camaraderie, and support the Trust's important work. International players representing Welsh rugby from 1950 to the present day, along with some of the injured players, have been delighted to share their favourite recipes in this book.

Thank you to everyone who has contributed to this most worthwhile of causes.

INTRODUCTION • CYFLWYNIAD

BY WRU PRESIDENT AND CHAIRMAN OF THE WELSH RUGBY CHARITABLE TRUST, DENNIS GETHIN

The guiding principle of the Welsh Rugby Charitable Trust, set up in 1972, is to enhance the quality of life of players who have suffered severe injuries while playing rugby football. One of the founder members was Sir Tasker Watkins VC, who was a former Chairman of the Trust and President of the Welsh Rugby Union. I know how much the work of the Trust meant to him and that he would have supported the publication of *The Dragons' Kitchen* wholeheartedly. The Trustees are all volunteers and are truly committed to ensuring that the founding principles are maintained. Together they enable practical support, sometimes in the form of specially adapted vehicles and wheelchairs, and also provide social opportunities for the injured players and their families. On behalf of the Trustees I should like to thank the Duke of Cambridge, our Patron, for his wonderful support which is greatly appreciated by everyone. Our grateful thanks also go to the Welsh Rugby Union for their continued financial assistance.

Prif egwyddor Ymddiriedolaeth Elusennol Rygbi Cymru, a sefydlwyd yn 1972, yw gwella ansawdd bywyd chwaraewyr sydd wedi dioddef anafiadau difrifol wrth chwarae rygbi. Un o'r aelodau sefydlu oedd Syr Tasker Watkins VC a oedd yn Gyn-gadeirydd yr Ymddiriedolaeth a Llywydd Undeb Rygbi Cymru. Yr wyf yn gwybod beth oedd gwaith yr Ymddiriedolaeth yn ei olygu iddo ac y byddai wedi cefnogi cyhoeddi llyfr Cegin y Dreigiau yn fawr iawn. Mae'r Ymddiriedolwyr i gyd yn wirfoddolwyr ac yn wironeddol ymrwymedig i sicrhau bod yr egwyddorion sylfaenol yn cael eu cynnal. Gyda'i gilydd maent yn galluogi cefnogaeth ymarferol, weithiau ar ffurf cerbydau a chadeiriau olwyn sydd wedi'u haddasu'n arbennig, a hefyd wrth ddarparu cyfleoedd cymdeithasu ar gyfer y chwaraewyr sydd wedi eu hanafu a'u teuluoedd. Ar ran yr Ymddiriedolwyr hoffwn ddiolch i Ddug Caergrawnt, ein Noddwr, am ei gefnogaeth wych sy'n cael ei gwerthfawrogi'n fawr gan bawb. Ein diolch hefyd i Undeb Rygbi Cymru am ei gymorth ariannol parhaus.

SHAUN PARRY-JONES

Shaun Parry-Jones was injured playing rugby in 1980.

Shaun Parry-Jones is one of the Trust's longest-standing beneficiaries. In 1980 Shaun was playing for Llandovery College against Ampleforth in the quarter-finals of the National Schoolboy 7's at Rosslyn Park. He tackled an opponent and fell awkwardly. Shaun broke his neck and is now tetraplegic, but he is still a great fan of the game.

"When something like this happens to you there is great trepidation about the future. How will you cope? What will you do? How on earth can you fund the care and equipment you need? Where will you live? Thirty years ago disability was viewed quite differently. Would I work? I certainly didn't expect to.

The support that I received from the Trust from the outset was incredible. Trustees visited me in Stoke Mandeville hospital to assure me that I would not be forgotten and said that if there was anything I needed I was only to ask. The Trust has moved on. No longer do you have to ask, they ask you. One of the Trustees is appointed to keep an eye on your circumstances and make sure that you are being catered for.

After hospital I went to university to study History of Art and Architecture. Art was something that I enjoyed. I did not think to study a vocational degree as it was unlikely, in those days, to result in employment. Having got my degree I decided to set up my own art business. I was very proud to show one of the Trustees the gallery I had set up.

However, it was not practical to run a gallery from a wheelchair and after seven years I decided to change tack. I was going back to university to study law. I am not sure that it would have been possible without the support of the Trust. I got through and had to move home in order to complete a training contract with a law firm. Again, the Trustees helped.

The Trust has always been a willing supporter, not only from a financial point of view but also in a pastoral role. If ever you need to talk to someone, the Trustees are only a phone call away. Events are organised for injured players to get together, which is an opportunity to catch up with the Trustees. Nothing is too much trouble.

Having an accident of this nature is scary, but life is less daunting when you know there is a safety net there to catch you should you get into difficulty. I am extremely grateful to the Trust for everything that it has done for me, knowing the support is there should you need it is very comforting."

PAUL DAVIES, MBE

Paul Davies: "The Trust is like having a kindly big brother."

"The Welsh Rugby Charitable Trust has been a big part of my life since my rugby injury in 1984. The Trust was formed to ensure the lives of players, severely injured through rugby, are made better. Their unstinting dedication to the welfare of each and every injured player is very reassuring; it's almost like having a kindly big brother watching over you. The Trustees are always very approachable and willing to listen to any problem I may have. I know I can approach them not just for financial matters but any help or advice I need on life in general.

They are constantly canvassing the views of the injured players themselves, all with a view to improving the way they run the Trust. As they are constantly reminding us, "They exist for us and our wellbeing" and they are very true to their word.

They make sure that we know we are not alone with our disability and ensure that all players get together at social functions etc whenever possible.

Thanks to the Trust I have the equipment I need to make my life in a wheelchair liveable. Personally, without the Trust in my life I would not have been able to do half the things I have been able to do, including travelling the world and enjoying playing sport at international level.

Over the years I have come to see them not as Trustees of a charity but firm friends, reliable, there to lend an ear and always willing to give advice and help where necessary and when needed."

WELSH RUGBY CHARITABLE TRUST – INJURED PLAYERS, 2014

Collin Smith, 49: Injured playing for Tonyrefail Comprehensive School (aged 15)

Richard Vowles, 41: Injured playing for Llanharan RFC (aged 24)

Shaun Parry-Jones, 54: Injured playing for Llandovery College (aged 19)

Carwyn Owen, 55: Injured playing for Old Palmerians RFC (aged 23)

Steve Harris, 62: Injured playing for Uxbridge RFC (aged 30)

Steve Coles, 43: Injured playing for Abergavenny RFC (aged 40)

Fran Bateman, 33: Injured playing for Gwernyfed RFC (aged 30)

Anthony Welsh, 57: Injured playing for Bedwas RFC (aged 35)

Bryan Wright, 34: Injured playing for Garndiffaith RFC (aged 32)

Wynn Francis, 62: Injured playing for Llanidloes RFC (aged 33)

Andrew Lewis, 43: Injured playing for Brecon RFC (aged 22)

Philip Harris, 61: Injured playing for Ystrad Rhondda RFC (aged 32)

Ceri Waters, 41: Injured playing for Cardigan RFC (aged 21)

Paul Flower, 38: Injured playing for Pontyclun RFC (aged 18)

Keith Walker, 52: Injured playing in a charity match (aged 25)

Robert Davies, 30: Injured playing for Brecon RFC (aged 21)

Malcolm Stephens, 53: Injured playing for Tumble RFC (aged 17)

Sion Maiden, 42: Injured playing for Machynlleth RFC (aged 19)

Paul Knight, 55: Rugby-related medical condition

Tim Green, 54: Injured playing for Pontyates RFC (aged 27)

Anthony James, 50: Injured playing for Monsanto RFC (aged 24)

Paul O'Keefe, 33: Injured playing for Aberavon Green Stars RFC (aged 18)

Dan Jones, 45: Injured playing for Newtown RFC (aged 20)

Victor Morris, 54: Injured playing for Lampeter RFC (aged 28)

Kevin Thomas, 49: Injured playing for Rhydyfelin RFC (aged 17)

Robert Moore, 51: Injured playing for Penallta RFC (aged 32)

Iwan Griffiths, 56: Injured playing for Glais RFC (aged 22)

Paul Davies, 52: Injured playing for Army XV (aged 21)

WARM UP
Starters and Soups

GARETH EDWARDS'
VICHYSSOISE VERT

Serves 4

250g **floury potatoes**
(Maris Piper or King
Edward), peeled and
chopped
250g **fresh** or **frozen peas**
6 **spring onions**, chopped
1 sprig **mint**, plus extra for
serving
1l **chicken stock**
15g **butter**
15g **cornflour**
300ml **whole milk**
50ml **double cream**

1 Place the potatoes, peas, spring onions, sprig of mint and stock in a large saucepan. Bring to the boil and simmer gently for 30 minutes until the potatoes are cooked.

2 Ladle the mixture into a blender or food processor and process until smooth, then return to the saucepan (or use a handheld blender to process in the saucepan). Season to taste with salt and ground black pepper.

3 Melt the butter in a small saucepan, then stir in the cornflour and add the milk slowly until it becomes a smooth sauce. Add this to the soup, stir well and heat through for about 2–3 minutes until you have a thickened, creamy soup. If serving hot, ladle into warm serving bowls and serve with a swirl of double cream and a sprinkle of chopped mint. Alternatively, leave to cool and place in the fridge before serving cold with a swirl of double cream and chopped mint.

> ❝ I first experienced and fell in love with this dish when I played my first game against France in 1967. The last international match I played was also against France in 1978, so it has special significance for me. It has been 47 years since I first tried it and my lovely wife makes it for me regularly. ❞

Gareth Edwards: Cap number: 711 **Career:** 1967–78 (53 caps)

ALAN PHILLIPS'
FRIED SCALLOPS AND BLACK PUDDING
with lemon and thyme dressing

Serves 2 as a starter

2 **parsnips**, peeled and chopped
¼ tsp **nutmeg**, freshly grated
2 tbsp **honey**
30g unsalted **butter**
50ml **single cream**
200g **black pudding**
1 tbsp **rapeseed oil**
6 **king scallops**

For the dressing:
1 tsp **English mustard**
1 tsp **caster sugar**
2 tbsp **rapeseed oil**
1 tsp **lemon juice**
1 tsp **thyme**, finely chopped, plus a few extra sprigs to serve

1 Place the parsnips in a medium saucepan, cover with boiling water and cook for 15 minutes until really soft. Drain well, then return to the pan and mash well until very smooth. Add a little grated nutmeg, the honey, butter and cream, and beat until smooth. Set aside.

2 Make the dressing by combining the mustard, sugar and a pinch of sea salt in a small bowl. Whisk in the oil, lemon juice and finely chopped thyme.

3 Slice the black pudding into rounds about the same thickness as a pound coin. Heat a frying pan until very hot, then add the oil and cook the black pudding and scallops for 2 minutes on each side until the scallops are golden.

4 Spoon the parsnip mash onto two warm plates and place the black pudding and scallops on top. Drizzle over the dressing, add a sprig of thyme and serve.

TIP: If you do not like black pudding then this recipe also works really well with chorizo sausage.

> This is a firm favourite in our home. It's shown here as a starter, but it also makes a fantastic main course too – you just get to enjoy a bigger portion!

Alan Phillips: Cap number: 782 **Career:** 1979–82 (15 caps)

BRYNMOR WILLIAMS'
LEEK AND POTATO SOUP

Serves 4

4 large **leeks**
50g unsalted **butter**
2 medium-sized **potatoes** (about 250g), peeled and chopped
1 medium **onion**, finely chopped
900ml **chicken stock**
300ml **whole milk**
2 tbsp **double cream**
2 tbsp **chives**, freshly chopped

1 Trim the leeks by removing the tops and tails. Split them in half lengthways and wash thoroughly, then pat dry with kitchen paper. Finely slice and set aside.

2 Melt the butter in a large, heavy-based saucepan. Add the leeks, potatoes and onions and stir into the butter until all the vegetables are well coated. Add a little salt and ground black pepper, then cover the pot and allow the vegetables to cook gently over a very low heat for about 15 minutes, stirring regularly.

3 Add the stock and milk and simmer gently for 20 minutes, with the pan uncovered, until the vegetables are very tender. Remove about half of the soup using a measuring jug and place in a liquidiser or food processor and blend until smooth. Return this to the soup so you have a texture which is half chunky vegetables and half smooth (alternatively, you can leave it all chunky or blend until smooth). Serve in warmed soup bowls with a sprinkling of chopped chives and an extra grinding of black pepper.

❝ Loving this dish all started with the raising of four sport-loving children, who were especially active with hockey, netball, football and rugby. My wife, Jayne, believed it was good for them to come home to a pot of hot, tasty soup and fresh brown bread to warm and fill them up in the winter months. In the early years it was Welsh cawl, but this leek and potato soup beats everything. I can't resist it, and when friends come round for dinner or the grown-up kids return home to visit they all ask for Jayne's 'L&P' soup. ❞

Brynmor Williams: Cap number: 772 **Career:** 1978–81 (3 caps)

J.P.R. WILLIAMS'
ROASTED BUTTERNUT SQUASH AND PARMA HAM SALAD

Serves 4

1 large **butternut squash**
2 tbsp **olive oil**
2 cloves **garlic**, finely chopped
1 large **red chilli**, finely chopped

20 slices **Parma ham**
50g **pine nuts**, toasted
70g **fresh rocket**
4 tbsp **balsamic vinegar**
4 tbsp **extra virgin olive oil**

1 Preheat the oven to 190C/375F/Gas 5. Cut the butternut squash in half, keeping the seeds intact and the skin on. Remove the ends and discard them. Cut each half into pieces approximately 8cm in length and 1.5cm thick and arrange in a large roasting tray. Pour over the olive oil and toss together well. Sprinkle with a little sea salt, ground black pepper and the chopped garlic and chilli, and toss again until all the squash is coated. Roast for about 1 hour and allow to cool.

2 In the meantime, arrange the Parma ham slices on four serving plates or a large serving platter in a criss-cross pattern. Let it dangle over the edge of the plates so it looks a little 'rustic'. Place chunks of the warm squash in and around the ham. Sprinkle the pine nuts and the rocket.

3 Drizzle over the balsamic vinegar and extra virgin olive oil, and finish with an extra grinding of ground black pepper. Serve immediately and enjoy!

TIP: If you are short on time, the butternut squash can be microwaved for about 10 minutes to help the cooking process. This should be done before any oil is added, then continue the recipe as above.

If you want to save time with chopping, you can use the jars of 'easy' ready-chopped garlic and chilli.

" I have always taken an interest in what I eat. I actually did my medical thesis on 'carbohydrate reloading' and I passed on a lot of what I knew to the other boys in the team. I think we were ahead of our time eating bread, potatoes and honey before matches, which was maybe one of the reasons for our success. "

J.P.R. Williams: Cap number: 729 **Career:** 1969–81 (55 caps)

MIKE HALL'S
BRUSCHETTA

Makes 12

6 large, ripe **plum tomatoes** (about 500g), chopped into 1.5cm cubes
1 **avocado**, halved, stone removed, peeled and chopped into 1.5cm cubes
4 tbsp **extra virgin olive oil**
1 handful **fresh basil**
400g **olive ciabatta bread**
1 clove **garlic**, halved
150g **cottage cheese**
6 slices **Parma ham**

1 Place the chopped tomatoes into a bowl and add the avocado, 2 tablespoons of extra virgin olive oil, basil leaves (reserving a few for garnish) and season well with a pinch of sea salt and a good grinding of black pepper.

2 Preheat the grill to high. Cut the bread into approximately 12 x 1.5cm thick slices and place under the grill to toast until golden. Remove the bread from the grill and immediately rub with the cut side of a clove of garlic (the warmth of the bread releases the garlic's aroma). Drizzle over the remaining extra virgin olive oil.

3 Spread a teaspoon of cottage cheese onto each piece of toasted bread, add half a slice of Parma ham, then finally top with a heaped tablespoon of the tomato and avocado mixture. Serve on a platter scattered with fresh basil leaves and add an extra grinding of black pepper.

Mike Hall: Cap number: 852 **Career:** 1988–95 (42 caps)

RICHARD VOWLES'
MUSHROOM SOUP

Serves 4

25g **butter**
1 tbsp **sunflower oil**
2 large **onions**, finely chopped
2 cloves **garlic**, finely chopped
300g **chestnut mushrooms**, chopped
300g **button mushrooms**, chopped
1l **chicken stock**
4 tbsp **double cream**
2 tbsp **flat leaf parsley**, finely chopped

1 Heat the butter and oil in a large, heavy-based saucepan, then add the onions and cook for about 10 minutes. Add the mushrooms (it will seem like a lot, but they will wilt down as they cook). Cook for a good 20 minutes, stirring every now and then until the mushrooms are golden and most of the moisture has evaporated. Add the garlic and cook for a few minutes longer.

2 Add the stock and simmer for a further 20 minutes and then blend (using a food processor or handheld blender) to your required consistency. You may need to add more water.

3 When ready, serve the soup with a warm baguette and lashings of butter. You can even add a swirl of fresh double cream, a sprinkling of flat leaf parsley and extra ground black pepper.

❝ This is quite nostalgic for us. We have a very young family and nothing beats sitting in front of our log fire on a cold winter's day with a nice bowl of mushroom soup and some fresh bread. It's so simple to make and is so versatile. It makes a great starter, but is also lovely served as a warming lunch or supper dish. ❞

Richard Vowles: Injured player

SHAUN PARRY-JONES'
PRAWN AND CRAYFISH TAIL SALAD
with avocado and mango

Serves 4 as a starter

2 ripe **avocados**, halved, stone removed, peeled and chopped into 1cm cubes

1 **mango**, peeled and chopped into 1cm cubes

1 **lemon**, halved

2 tbsp **salad cream**

2 tbsp **tomato ketchup**

2 tbsp **mayonnaise**

2 **little gem lettuce**, sliced very thinly

30g **fresh rocket**

200g cooked **king prawns** and **crayfish tails**

2 tbsp **chives**, freshly chopped

1 Place the avocado and mango into a bowl and squeeze half the lemon over the mixture to retain the colour.

2 Mix the salad cream, tomato ketchup and mayonnaise in a separate bowl. Add a grinding of black pepper to taste.

3 Mix the shredded lettuce and rocket leaves together and place into the bottom of small bowls, large glasses or 1920s cocktail glasses (as we do!)

4 Spoon the avocado and mango mixture on top of the lettuce, then divide the prawns and crayfish between the glasses. Spoon the dressing on top, then take the remaining lemon and slice it into four and place on top of each serving.

5 Finally, sprinkle with chopped chives. Wonderful with a little rye bread on the side. Not too difficult or complicated, but delicious!

" One of my favourite starters in the 1970s/80s was a prawn cocktail. In fact, I continue to enjoy a prawn cocktail today. However, my wife, Lesley, has brought the starter into the 21st century. I call it a starter, but it is actually something we enjoy together as a light lunch in the summer. Whenever we are entertaining friends, usually related to rugby in some guise or another, Lesley's fresh take on this 1970s favourite is often the most popular aspect of the meal. "

Shaun Parry-Jones: Injured player

JAMIE ROBERTS'
CAPRESE SALAD

Serves 4 as a starter or 2 as a main course

4 large, ripe **tomatoes**, sliced
2 x 125g balls **buffalo mozzarella**, sliced
12 large **basil** leaves, roughly torn
2 tbsp **extra virgin olive oil**
Ground **black pepper**
1 tbsp **balsamic vinegar**

1 Choose only the best, seasonal ingredients for this recipe. Make sure you use the best of the season's tomatoes that you can find. Smell them before buying and they should have a powerful aroma, but whatever you do don't put them in the fridge, and instead keep them in a bowl at room temperature. The mozzarella must be soft. Look out for the buffalo variety as this has a soft, creamy and fresh taste and texture. Again, in the summer months basil has a much more peppery flavour and a wonderful aroma.

2 Place the sliced tomatoes and mozzarella alternately on a plate. Dress with the basil leaves, black pepper and the olive oil. Drizzle with the balsamic vinegar and serve with crusty bread.

Jamie Roberts: Cap number: 1057 **Career:** 2008– (60 caps)

DENNIS GETHIN'S
THE PRESIDENT'S SPICY SWEET POTATO SOUP

Serves 6

500g **sweet potatoes** or **yams**
500g **fresh tomatoes**, skinned and roughly chopped
50g **butter**
1 medium **onion**, finely chopped
1 or 2 **fresh red chillies**, deseeded and finely chopped (depending on how spicy and hot you like your food)
1l **chicken stock**
2 tbsp **fresh coriander**, chopped
1 tbsp **crème fraîche** or thick **Greek-style yoghurt** (optional)

1 Peel and slice the sweet potatoes and put them into a large saucepan with enough salted water to cover them. Bring to the boil, cover and cook for about 20 minutes until tender. Drain into a colander and chop into smaller chunks. Set aside. (No need to wash the saucepan, as you will use it again in a moment.)

2 Melt the butter in a frying pan over a low heat and gently fry the onion until soft but not browned (approximately 10 minutes). Then add the chopped tomatoes and any juices, plus the chillies, and cook for a further 5 minutes.

3 Transfer the contents of the frying pan into a blender or food processor and add the cooked sweet potatoes. Add 225ml of the chicken stock and blend until smooth.

4 Transfer the puréed mixture back into the saucepan you used to boil the sweet potatoes and add the remaining chicken stock. Check the seasoning and add salt if necessary, plus black pepper to taste. Add half the chopped coriander. Simmer very gently over a low heat for about 5 minutes. Pour into warmed serving bowls and add a spoonful of crème fraîche/ yoghurt (optional) and a sprinkling of the remaining fresh coriander.

Dennis Gethin: President of the Welsh Rugby Union and Chairman of the Welsh Rugby Charitable Trust

SCRUM DOWN
Main Courses

JONATHAN DAVIES'
JIFFY'S TRADITIONAL WELSH BREAKFAST

Serves 2

1 tbsp **sunflower oil**
6 rashers unsmoked back **bacon**
2 large free-range **eggs**
100g **laverbread**
150g **fresh cockles**

1 Heat a frying pan and add the sunflower oil. Cook the bacon for about 3 minutes each side until golden and crispy. Transfer to two serving plates and keep warm in a low oven.

2 Add the laverbread and cockles to the frying pan, cook for just a few minutes and then spoon onto the plates.

3 Wipe the frying pan clean and pour in boiling water from the kettle to just fill. Bring to a very gentle simmer and then crack in 2 eggs and poach for 3–4 minutes. Spoon onto the serving plates, draining away any excess water on kitchen paper. Serve with toasted crusty bread.

" Growing up, I used to pick the cockles on the beach and buy the laverbread from either Llanelli or Swansea market. This was our breakfast and it is still a firm favourite for me. I still look for this combination when I go out to any of the local Welsh restaurants. "

Jonathan Davies: Cap number: 827 **Career:** 1985–97 (32 caps)

SAM WARBURTON'S
CHILLI CON CARNE
with cherry tomato salad

Serves 4

For the chilli con carne:
1 tbsp **olive oil**
1 **onion**, finely chopped
2 cloves **garlic**, finely chopped
1 tbsp **smoked paprika**
1 tbsp **hot chilli powder**
500g **minced beef**
1 **red pepper**, halved, deseeded and diced
1 **green pepper**, halved, deseeded and diced
1 **green chilli**, finely chopped
2 tbsp **tomato purée**
400g can **chopped tomatoes**
400g can **kidney beans**, drained
1 handful **fresh coriander**, chopped

To serve:
100g mixed **salad leaves**
150g **cherry tomatoes**, halved
200g mixed **basmati** and **wild rice**
50g **mature cheddar cheese**, grated
4 tbsp **soured cream**

1 Heat the oil in a large saucepan and cook the onion for a few minutes until they begin to soften, then stir in the garlic and cook for 1 minute longer. Add the spices and cook for 1 minute.

2 Stir in the minced beef and brown all over, then add the peppers and chopped chilli and cook for about 2 minutes.

3 Stir in the tomato purée and cook for 1 minute, then add the chopped tomatoes and bring to a simmer. Cook for 30–40 minutes and then stir in the kidney beans and fresh coriander.

4 Serve with the salad leaves and cherry tomatoes, the basmati and wild rice and extras such as grated cheese and soured cream.

❝ Chilli con carne is my favourite meal because it's high in protein and carbohydrates, which is essential for my training. It's my preferred meal to have the night before a game. The only problem with chilli con carne is that I eat it so often that I have to wait until my wife is out of the house because she is tired of eating the same meal! **❞**

Sam Warburton: **Cap number:** 1070 **Career:** 2009– (46 caps)

NEIL JENKINS'
CHARGRILLED STEAK AND CHIPS

Serves 4

3 large **baking potatoes**,
peeled and cut into thick chips
1 1/2l **groundnut oil** (for deep
frying)
4 **rump steaks** (approximately
150g each)
2 tbsp **olive oil**
4 large **tomatoes**
4 sprigs **flat leaf parsley**

1 Prepare the chips first. Bring a saucepan of water to the boil and add the prepared potatoes. Parboil for 4–5 minutes, drain well and pat dry with kitchen paper.

2 Fill a medium-sized saucepan two-thirds full with the groundnut oil and heat until hot. To test if the oil is hot enough, drop a piece of bread into the oil and, if it turns brown in a few seconds, it is ready. Carefully lower the chips into the oil and cook for 1–2 minutes until golden and crispy on the outside and fluffy in the middle. Remove from the pan with a slotted spoon onto kitchen paper to drain. When dry, place the chips in the oven on a low temperature to keep warm and crispy while you prepare the steaks.

3 Heat a griddle pan until smoking hot. Rub a little of the olive oil over the steaks and season well with salt and freshly ground black pepper. Griddle the steaks for 3–4 minutes on each side (for rare) or until cooked to your liking, then remove from the pan and allow to rest on a warm plate.

4 Cut the tomatoes in half and drizzle with the remaining olive oil. Place cut side down on the hot griddle and cook for 2–3 minutes until softened and slightly charred.

5 Serve the steak with the chips and tomatoes, and garnish with some fresh parsley.

" This might not be the most complicated recipe in this book, but it is certainly my favourite. I don't like fancy food and I can honestly say that I have tried this dish all over the world and it is still my favourite! **"**

Neil Jenkins: Cap number: 890 **Career:** 1991–2002 (87 caps)

Warren Gatland is pictured cooking his herb crusted lamb for his coaching team, including Huw Bennett (*above, second from the left*, who was enlisted as his assistant), Neil Jenkins, Alan Phillips and Robin McBryde (*above, far right*) and Rob Howley (*overleaf, far left*).

WARREN GATLAND'S
HERB CRUSTED LAMB RACK

Serves 2

For the herb crusted lamb:
1 **lamb rack**
1 tbsp **Dijon mustard**
1 clove **garlic**, crushed
1 tbsp **thyme**, finely chopped
1 tbsp **flat leaf parsley**, finely chopped
1 tbsp **mint**, finely chopped
2 tbsp **pine nuts**, finely chopped
Zest ½ **lemon**

For the stuffed lamb:
1 **lamb rack**
30g **butter**

1 tbsp **flat leaf parsley**, finely chopped
1 tbsp **thyme**, finely chopped
1 tbsp **mint**, finely chopped

For the mash:
2 **potatoes**, peeled and diced
1 **sweet potato**, peeled and diced
2 cloves **garlic**, crushed
100ml **double cream**
30g **butter**

For the pea purée:
50g **butter**

2 **shallots**, finely diced
100g **frozen peas**
100ml **vegetable stock**
1 small handful **mint**

For the baby carrots:
8 **baby carrots**, cleaned
30g **butter**
1 tbsp **honey**

For the red wine sauce:
2 **shallots**, chopped
1 clove **garlic**, chopped
200ml **red wine**
1 tbsp **balsamic vinegar**
1 sprig **rosemary**
1 **bay leaf**
100g **butter**, cubed

> On one of my recent visits back home, I took part in a charity auction where I was part of the prize! I was required to cook dinner for a group of friends and this is the dish I chose. It was one of the recipes featured on *NZ Masterchef*, which was really good because I could watch precisely how it was done!

1 Preheat the oven to 180C/356F/Gas 4. Drizzle the lamb rack with olive oil and season with salt and pepper. Combine the garlic, thyme, parsley, mint, pine nuts and lemon zest in a bowl. Spread the mustard over the meat, then coat in the herbs. Place on a baking tray.

2 For the stuffed lamb, combine the butter, parsley, thyme and mint in a bowl. Make an incision between the meat and bones and stuff with the butter. Place on the baking tray and cook in the oven for 15–25 minutes or until cooked to your liking. Rest for 10 minutes.

3 Meanwhile, make the mash by placing the potatoes, sweet potato and garlic in a saucepan, cover with salted water and place over a high heat. Bring to the boil, then reduce to a simmer and cook for 10–12 minutes or until tender. Drain well and mash with the cream and butter until smooth and creamy.

4 For the pea purée, heat a frying pan over a medium heat and add the butter and shallots and sauté until soft. Add the peas, stock and mint leaves and cook for 5–8 minutes until the peas are soft but still green. Drain, but keep the cooking liquid and put it to one side. Place the shallots and peas into a blender and blend into a purée, adding the cooking liquid to help purée. Season with salt and pepper.

5 For the baby carrots, bring a saucepan of salted water to the boil. Reduce to a simmer and add the carrots and cook for 4–8 minutes or until tender. Drain and return to the saucepan, add butter and honey and cook until lightly caramelised, then season with salt and pepper.

6 For the red wine sauce, heat an oiled frying pan over a medium heat and cook the shallots and garlic for 1–2 minutes until soft. Add the red wine, balsamic, rosemary and bay leaf and reduce by half, then season with salt and pepper. Remove from heat, strain through a sieve into a clean saucepan and whisk in the butter a small amount at a time to make a thick, glossy sauce.

7 To serve, spoon the pea purée over the serving plate, then top with slices of the herb crusted lamb rack and the stuffed lamb. Place the baby carrots to one side with a spoon of mash, then spoon over the red wine sauce.

Warren Gatland's dish is inspired by the winning recipe from the New Zealand edition of **Masterchef**

PHIL BENNETT'S
CORNED BEEF PLAIT

Serves 4-6

500g **floury potatoes** (Maris Piper or King Edward)
340g can **corned beef**, mashed
1 small **onion**, finely chopped
300g can **mixed vegetables**, drained
1 tsp **dried thyme**
500g ready-made **puff pastry**
1 tbsp **plain flour**
1 medium **egg**, beaten

1 Preheat the oven to 200C/390F/Gas 6. Line a large baking tray with parchment paper. Peel and chop the potatoes, then place in a large saucepan and cover with water. Bring to the boil and simmer for 15–20 minutes until very soft. Drain well, return to the pan and mash until smooth. Season with a little salt and some ground black pepper. Transfer to a bowl and leave to cool.

2 When the potatoes have cooled, stir in the mashed corned beef, onion, mixed vegetables and dried thyme, and mix everything together with a fork.

3 Roll out the puff pastry on a lightly floured surface to measure approximately 30cm x 30cm.

Place the pastry on the lined baking tray. Lay the filling down the centre of the pastry (just like making a sausage roll), leaving a 3cm gap of pastry at each end.

4 Cut the pastry on either side of the filling at a slight diagonal into 12 x 1.5cm strips, making sure you cut the same number each side.

5 Tuck the top and bottom edges of the pastry over the filling. Starting at the top, lay the pastry strips over the filling, taking one from each side, to cross like a plait. Brush all over with the beaten egg and bake for 35 minutes until golden brown. Leave to cool for 10 minutes before serving.

Phil Bennett: Cap number: 730 **Career:** 1969-79 (29 caps)

DEREK & SCOTT QUINNELL'S
BEEF WITH WHISKY

Serves 4

2 tbsp **olive oil**
1 large **onion**, finely chopped
6 rashers **bacon**, cut into strips
2–3 tbsp **whisky**
1kg **braising steak**, cut into 3cm cubes
30g **plain flour**
600ml **beef stock**
300ml **red wine**
2 tbsp **fresh flat leaf parsley**, chopped

1 Preheat the oven to 150C/300F/Gas 3. Heat a tablespoon of the oil in a heavy-based casserole dish and add the onions and the strips of bacon. Cook for about 5–7 minutes until the onions are softened and the bacon is golden. Add the whisky and flambé by igniting the alcohol and allowing the flame to die down. Remove the onions and bacon from the pan and set aside.

2 Place the beef in a bowl and add the flour and a good pinch of salt and ground black pepper.

3 Heat the remaining oil in the casserole dish and cook the beef for a few minutes until browned all over. Stir in the wine, beef stock and reserved onions and bacon. Cover with a lid and cook in the oven for approximately 2 hours until the meat is meltingly tender and the sauce is thickened and glossy.

4 Serve with creamy mashed potatoes and green beans and sprinkle with chopped flat leaf parsley.

" Beef in whisky is a fairly new recipe which Madora [Mam] introduced at a Boxing Day family gathering at Scott and Nicola's home. It proved so popular that it is now a regular for us throughout the year. " **Derek Quinnell**

Derek Quinnell: Cap number: 744 **Career:** 1972-79 (23 caps)
Scott Quinnell: Cap number: 911 **Career:** 1993-02 (52 caps)

ADAM JONES'
PULLED PORK WITH SPICY COLESLAW

Serves 6

For the pulled pork:
2kg **pork shoulder**
1 tbsp **chilli flakes**
2 tbsp **wholegrain mustard**
500ml bottle **dry cider**
3 **onions**, finely chopped
6 cloves **garlic**, chopped

For the coleslaw:
½ **white cabbage**, finely chopped
2 **carrots**, finely chopped
1 **red onion**, finely chopped
1 **red chilli**, finely chopped
3 tbsp **mayonnaise**
Juice 1 **lemon**

1 Preheat the oven to 170C/338F/Gas 3. Place the pork shoulder in a large roasting tin. Place the chilli flakes, mustard and a pinch of salt and ground black pepper in a bowl and mix together well. Rub the mixture over the pork. Pour the cider into the tin and add the onions and garlic. Cover with foil and place in the oven for 4 hours. The pork should be very tender and fall apart when you pull at it with a fork.

2 Place the cabbage, carrots, red onion and chilli in a large bowl and toss together well. Mix the mayonnaise, lemon juice and a pinch of salt together. Pour over the vegetables and mix.

3 Remove the pork from the oven and shred the meat into pieces using two forks. Toss in the roasting tin with the juices, onions and garlic.

4 Serve piled onto a warmed serving platter with the coleslaw, soft rolls and barbecue sauce.

❝ I'm always on the look out for a new dish and had been recommended to try pulled pork with spicy coleslaw. I spent an hour in the supermarket looking for the best ingredients to use and investigating to see if there was anything I could add to make the dish my own. I finally decided to opt for Welsh ingredients: Welsh pork, Welsh carrots, Welsh cider etc. After spending over an hour preparing the marinade, pork, vegetables for the coleslaw, measuring the right size of foil and greaseproof paper, and the next six hours waiting and smelling the most amazing smell ever, the pork was ready. It fell apart and I couldn't resist trying it – so much so that I burned my mouth! It has since become our family favourite. **❞**

Adam Jones: Cap number: 1018 **Career:** 2003– (95 caps)

MATTHEW REES'
CHICKEN CURRY

Serves 4

2 tbsp **vegetable oil**
2 **onions**, halved and finely chopped
6 **chicken breasts**, cut into 3cm cubes
3 **red** or **yellow peppers**, halved, deseeded and chopped
400g **chestnut mushrooms**, finely chopped
4 tbsp **Madras curry paste**
4 tbsp **mango chutney**
400ml **hot vegetable stock**
400g can **coconut milk**
2 tbsp **cornflour**

1 Heat the oil in a large frying pan and add the onions and cook for about 8 minutes until softened. Add the chicken to the pan and cook for a few minutes until lightly browned, then add the peppers and mushrooms and cook for 4–5 minutes. Add the madras curry paste and mango chutney and stir it all together, then add the stock and cook for a further 5 minutes.

2 Stir in the coconut milk and bring to the boil, then simmer gently for 10 minutes.

3 Mix the cornflour with 3 tablespoons of cold water and then add a little at a time to the pan until the curry thickens. Simmer for a further 5 minutes. Serve with rice, poppadoms and mango chutney.

Matthew Rees: Cap number: 1033 **Career:** 2005– (60 caps)

SCOTT GIBBS'
TURKEY AND VEAL MEATLOAF

Serves 4–6

2 tbsp **olive oil**
1 **shallot**, finely chopped
1 **carrot**, diced into 1cm cubes
1 **turnip**, diced into 1cm cubes
1 **leek**, chopped
1 tsp freshly ground **black pepper**
250g organic **turkey mince**
250g organic **veal mince**
400g can **lentils**, drained well

4 large handfuls of wilted **baby spinach** (about 200g)
1 tsp **fresh thyme**
1 tsp **Worcestershire sauce**
1 large **egg**, beaten
100g grated **parmesan**
A generous squeeze of **tomato ketchup**
3 large **hard-boiled eggs**

1 Heat the olive oil in a frying pan and add the shallot, carrot and turnip and cook on a medium heat for 5 minutes to soften, then add the leek and reduce to a low heat for another 5 minutes. Transfer the vegetables to a large mixing bowl and set aside to cool. Season with the black pepper and a pinch of salt to taste.

2 Add the turkey and veal mince to the vegetables and stir in well, then add the lentils. Squeeze out any excess liquid from the wilted spinach and chop roughly. Stir this into the mixture and add the thyme and Worcestershire sauce.

   Add the beaten egg, the parmesan cheese and squeeze a generous amount of tomato ketchup into the mix for one last fold and stir. Place the mixture in the fridge for 20 minutes to bind.

3 Preheat the oven to 180C/356F/Gas 4. Spoon half the mixture into a 1kg non-stick loaf tin and then place the boiled eggs upright in the centre of the filling. Add the remainder of the filling to the tin, pressing down gently on top. Place in the oven and bake for 45–50 minutes until the top is golden brown (drain excess juices if required). Leave to settle for 20 minutes, then turn out onto a chopping board and slice into thick wedges.

4 Eat hot or cold – it's beautiful both ways. Serve with a side salad of little gem or butter lettuce leaves, chopped avocado, sprinkled with toasted pine nuts and tossed with a lemon and Dijon mustard dressing. If you need some extra kick, pick up some Cholula (hot salsa).

Scott Gibbs: Cap number: 889 **Career:** 1991–01 (53 caps)

PAUL FLOWER'S
PAUL'S BALLS

Serves 4

For Paul's Balls:
500g good quality
Welsh minced beef
1 sprig **fresh rosemary**, finely chopped
1 handful **fresh parsley**, finely chopped
2 tbsp **olive oil**
100g **fresh breadcrumbs**
2 cloves **garlic**, finely chopped
1 **onion**, finely chopped

2 large **egg yolks**, beaten
2 tsp **Dijon mustard**
75g **medium cheddar cheese**

For the tomato sauce:
2 tbsp **olive oil**
1 clove **garlic**, finely chopped
2 x 400g cans **chopped tomatoes**

1 Place the beef mince into a large mixing bowl with the chopped rosemary and parsley.

2 Heat 1 tablespoon of olive oil in a frying pan, then add the garlic and breadcrumbs and cook over a gentle heat until the breadcrumbs are golden and crunchy. Add these to the bowl with the mince.

3 Add the onion, egg yolks and mustard to the mixture and mix well, seasoning with a pinch of salt and plenty of ground black pepper.

4 Cut the cheddar cheese into 1cm cubes. Take a handful of the minced meat mixture and wrap it around a cube of cheese and shape into a meatball. Repeat until all the mixture has been used.

5 Heat the remaining olive oil in the frying pan and cook the meatballs for a few minutes until browned all over. Set aside.

6 Make a simple tomato sauce by heating the olive oil in a large casserole dish or saucepan and add the garlic slices and cook for 30 seconds. Tip in the chopped tomatoes and simmer for about 10 minutes, then add the meatballs and transfer to the oven and bake slowly for about 45 minutes. Serve with tagliatelle pasta.

Alternatively: Fry on a low heat until cooked through, then serve on chapati bread, with fried parsnip shavings and a mild horseradish mayonnaise.

 My recipe inspiration evolved through trying to introduce my son to cheese. He loved meatballs but hated cheese, so by hiding cheese within the meatballs (much like we do by hiding vegetables in soup) we discovered it was a success. Hence, 'Paul's Balls' was born – sneaky, but effective! ""

Paul Flower: Injured player

LEIGH HALFPENNY'S
WELSH LAMB CAWL

Serves 6

1 tbsp **sunflower oil**

6 **lamb shanks**

1 **onion**, chopped

2 **leeks**, halved and chopped

1 large **potato**, peeled and cut into 1cm cubes

300g **swede**, peeled and cut into 1cm cubes

300g **carrots**, peeled and cut into 1cm cubes

1 **bay leaf**

2 sprigs **rosemary**

2 sprigs **fresh thyme**

2l **vegetable stock**

2 tbsp **fresh flat leaf parsley**, chopped

1 Preheat the oven to 170C/338F/Gas 3. Heat the sunflower oil in a large ovenproof casserole dish and add the lamb shanks a few at a time and cook until browned all over. Set aside.

2 Add the onion and leek to the casserole dish and cook for about 5 minutes until softened and golden. Stir in the potato, swede and carrots and cook for a further 5 minutes. Add the bay leaf, rosemary and thyme to the vegetables and return the lamb shanks back to the dish. Pour over the stock and season with a little salt and ground black pepper. Cover and place in the oven for 2 hours until the lamb is meltingly tender.

3 Take the lamb out of the oven, remove the meat from the bone and return to the mixture.

4 Serve garnished with chopped parsley and with warm crusty bread and Caerphilly cheese.

Leigh Halfpenny: Cap number: 1060 **Career:** 2008– (52 caps)

BARRY JOHN'S
BEEF ORLANDO

Serves 4

2 tbsp **olive oil**
900g good quality
braising steak, cut into
cubes
2 large **onions**, sliced
400g can **chopped
tomatoes**
1 tsp **curry powder**
2 tbsp **tomato purée**
1 tbsp **white wine
vinegar**
2 tbsp **apricot preserve**
2 **bay leaves**
3 tbsp chopped **parsley**

1 Preheat the oven to 160C/320F/Gas 3. Heat
the olive oil in a large casserole dish and brown
the beef in batches in the hot oil to seal. Lower
the heat and add the onions, then fry together
for a few minutes.

2 Add the remaining ingredients to the pan,
except the parsley. Bring gently to the boil.
Cover with a lid and cook in the oven, stirring
occasionally, for about 2 hours until the meat is
tender and the sauce is reduced and thickened.

3 Garnish with parsley and serve with boiled
rice and a choice of seasonal vegetables.

Barry John: Cap number: 703 **Career:** 1966–72 (25 caps)

STEVE FENWICK'S
GRAND SLAM LAMB JALFREZI

Serves 4

For the curried onions:
1 tbsp **vegetable oil**
2 medium **onions**, finely chopped
½ tsp **paprika**
½ tsp ground **cardamom**
½ tsp ground **cloves**
½ tsp **garam masala**

For the lamb:
1 tbsp **vegetable oil**
1.5kg **lamb shoulder**, cut into 2cm cubes
1 large **onion**, finely chopped
2cm piece **root ginger**, finely chopped
4 cloves **garlic**, finely chopped
1 tsp **turmeric**
1 tsp **garam masala**
450g jar **jalfrezi sauce**
1 large handful **fresh coriander**, chopped

For the rice:
300g **long grain rice**
4 **cloves**
1 **cinnamon stick**
½ tsp **turmeric**
600ml **vegetable stock**
150g **fresh** or **frozen peas**
Juice ½ **lemon**

1 Cook the curried onions first. Heat the oil in a large frying pan, add the onions and cook for a few minutes until they begin to soften. Add the spices and cook very gently for a further 10 minutes until the onions are golden and very soft. Add a little water if the onions are cooking too quickly. Set aside.

2 For the lamb, heat the oil in the pan you have just cooked the onions in and cook the lamb cubes for a few minutes until browned all over. You may have to do this in batches. Remove the lamb from the pan and set aside. Add the chopped large onion to the pan and cook for a few minutes, then add the ginger and garlic and cook for 1 minute. Stir in the turmeric and garam masala and cook for 1 minute, tossing together well with the onions. Return the lamb to the pan

with the jar of jalfrezi sauce and bring to a gentle simmer. Cover and cook over a very gentle heat for 40–50 minutes until the lamb is very tender.

3 Meanwhile, whilst the lamb is cooking, place the rice in a saucepan with the cloves, cinnamon and turmeric and pour over the stock. Bring to a simmer and cook for 15–20 minutes until the rice has nearly absorbed all the liquid. Stir in the peas and simmer for a further 5 minutes until the rice is thoroughly cooked. Place a lid on top of the rice and leave to stand for 5 minutes.

4 Stir the curried onions into the lamb and add the chopped fresh coriander.

5 Stir the lemon juice into the rice and serve.

❝ This is something the family often cook at home in the evening, especially when the weather is cold and miserable outside. It's also great for when I have been away on tour or travelling extensively and haven't had an authentic curry for a while. **❞**

Steve Fenwick: Cap number: 762 **Career:** 1975-81 (30 caps)

ROB HOWLEY'S
SPAGHETTI BOLOGNESE

Serves 4

1 tbsp **olive oil**
1 large **onion**, finely chopped
2 cloves **garlic**, finely chopped or crushed
1 tsp **dried mixed herbs**

6 medium **mushrooms**, chopped
500g **mince beef**
70g **tomato purée**
1 tsp **sugar**
500ml **beef stock**

500g **spaghetti**
4 tbsp **flat leaf parsley**, chopped

1 Heat the olive oil in a large saucepan and cook the onion gently for 5 minutes until softened. Add the garlic and dried herbs and cook for a further minute.

Stir in the mushrooms and cook for a few minutes, then add the minced beef and brown all over, breaking it up in the pan with a wooden spoon. Brown for 5 minutes, then add the tomato purée, stir in well and cook for 1 minute. Add the sugar and stock and bring to a very gentle simmer. Cover and cook for 30 minutes, then remove the lid and continue for a further 20 minutes, stirring every now and then.

2 Bring a large pan of water to the boil and cook the spaghetti according to the packet instructions. Drain well and serve with the sauce and a sprinkling of chopped parsley.

" I wasn't a fan of spaghetti bolognese when I first met my wife. She asked me a few times if I wanted it for tea, but each time I said I didn't like it. One evening after I had come home from work, I was presented with minced beef in a tomato and mushroom sauce. After I had cleared my plate, my wife was looking very pleased with herself. 'You do like spaghetti bolognese,' she said, 'you've just eaten it! "

Row Howley: Cap number: 940 **Career:** 1996–2002 (59 caps)

HUW BENNETT'S
HOMEMADE TURKEY BURGERS

Makes 6 burgers

500g **turkey mince**
1 **shallot**, finely chopped
2 tbsp **whole wheat breadcrumbs**
1 clove **garlic**, crushed
1 **red chilli**, finely chopped (optional)
1 large **egg**, beaten
2 **gem lettuce**, leaves separated and washed
4 **tomatoes**, finely chopped
½ **cucumber**, finely chopped
1 **red pepper**, halved, deseeded and finely chopped
1 **yellow pepper**, halved, deseeded and finely chopped
100g **mature cheddar cheese**, finely chopped or grated
6 **burger buns**

1 Place the turkey, chopped shallot, breadcrumbs, garlic and chilli (optional) in a bowl and mix together well. Mix in the egg to bind. Place in the fridge to chill for about 30 minutes – this makes them easier to handle.

2 With wet hands, shape the mixture into 6 burgers and either place under a hot grill for about 8–10 minutes each side or on the barbecue.

3 Serve in burger buns with a choice of accompaniments including lettuce, tomatoes, cucumber, peppers and cheese.

" With three children in the house it's fun to get them involved with this simple recipe. We call it 'burger night' and, after we make our own burgers, we then build our burgers at the table using the extras such as lettuce, tomatoes, cucumber, cheese and peppers. It's a little trick we use to make it more fun for the kids and, as they add their own vegetables, to give them more of a varied diet without them knowing it. "

Huw Bennett: Cap number: 1017 **Career:** 2003–13 (51 caps)

DWAYNE PEEL'S
LOBSTER CANNELLONI

Serves 4

For the pasta:
1 pinch **saffron**
250g **Tipo 'OO' flour**
1 medium **egg**

For the shellfish sauce:
1 tbsp **olive oil**
25g **onions**, finely chopped
25g **carrots**, finely chopped
25g **leeks**, finely chopped
25g **celery**, finely chopped
500g **lobster** and **crab shells**
100ml **brandy**
5g **tomato purée**
250ml **double cream**

For the mousse:
100g **salmon fillet**
50g **scallop meat**
1 **egg white**
200ml **double cream**
400g **lobster meat**, chopped
2 tbsp **parsley**, finely chopped, plus extra for garnish
1 small bunch **chives**, finely chopped

1 To make the pasta, place the saffron in a bowl with 100ml of boiling water and leave to stand for 10 minutes. Place the flour in a food processor with a good pinch of salt and then add the egg and saffron stock and process until the mixture forms a soft dough. Knead on a lightly floured work surface for about 5 minutes, then wrap in cling film and leave to rest for 4 hours.

2 Meanwhile, make the shellfish sauce. Heat the oil in a large saucepan and add the onions, carrot, celery and leeks and cook gently for 8 minutes until softened. Add the lobster and crab shells, turn up the heat and pour in the brandy. Simmer rapidly for a few minutes to evaporate the alcohol. Reduce the heat and then add the tomato purée and cook for 10 minutes. Cover with water, bring to the boil and simmer for 20 minutes. Strain the sauce through a sieve, return to the saucepan and simmer for a further 10 minutes until reduced by half. Add the cream and heat for 10 minutes. Check seasoning and set aside.

3 To make the mousse filling, place the salmon and scallop meat in a blender and process until smooth. Add the egg white and season with a little salt. Pour in the double cream slowly and then transfer to a bowl and stir in the lobster meat and parsley. Spoon into a large piping bag with a large nozzle measuring about 1.5cm. Set aside in the fridge whilst you prepare the pasta.

4 Roll out the pasta in a pasta machine down to number 1. Roll twice on number 1 then cut into eight oblongs measuring approximately 5cm x 12cm. Bring a pan of water to the boil and cook the pasta for just a minute, then drain and refresh in cold water.

5 Lay the pasta oblongs on sheets of cling film. Pipe the lobster mousse along the width of the pasta, roll up the pasta tightly and then wrap in the cling film and tie securely at both ends. Repeat with the remaining pasta and filling.

6 Place the pasta parcels in boiling water for 10 minutes. Remove from the cling film and serve two cannelloni per person with the warmed shellfish sauce. Garnish with chives and a little parsley.

Recipe reproduced with the kind permission of the Sosban restaurant, Llanelli

Dwayne Peel: Cap number: 994 **Career:** 2001– (76 caps)

IEUAN EVANS'
KING PRAWN LINGUINE

Serves 5 in the Evans household

550g **fresh** or **dried linguine**
2 tbsp **extra virgin olive oil**, plus extra for serving
3 cloves **garlic**, finely chopped or crushed
1 **red chilli**, finely chopped
300g **cherry** or **pomodorino tomatoes**
150g **button mushrooms**, halved
1 large **red pepper**, halved, deseeded and sliced
400g raw **king prawns**
30g **fresh rocket**
4 tbsp grated **parmesan**

1 Bring a large saucepan of salted water to the boil and cook the linguine according to the instructions until *al dente*. Drain and put to one side.

2 Heat a large frying pan or wok and add the oil. Stir in the garlic and chilli and cook for 1 minute, then add the tomatoes, mushrooms and peppers and toss well with the oil, garlic and chillies. Cook for 3 minutes until the vegetables are tender, stirring all the time. Finally, add the prawns and cook for 3–4 minutes until pink and cooked through.

3 Add the linguine to the pan and toss well, then add the parmesan, rocket and a few extra glugs of olive oil. Toss well over a low heat to ensure the linguine absorbs the lovely, hot, garlic- and tomato-flavoured oil.

4 Add more rocket, parmesan, salt and pepper to taste and voila! Serve with a large glass of Sauvignon Blanc, Sancerre or Chablis.

" Seafood is one of my favourite food types and this recipe is super-quick, nutritious and tastes gorgeous too. A great favourite with the Evans family and one worth trying. "

Ieuan Evans: Cap number: 836 **Career:** 1987-98 (72 caps)

MARTYN WILLIAMS'
NUGGET'S FAMILY FISH PIE

Serves 4

600g **potatoes**, peeled and chopped
100g **butter**
500ml **whole milk**
300g **cod fillets**, skinned
300g **salmon fillets**, skinned
50g **flour**
150g **frozen peas**
2 tbsp **fresh parsley**, chopped
2 tsp **lemon juice**
2 **hard-boiled eggs**, chopped
25g **mature cheddar cheese**, grated

1 Preheat the oven to 180C/350F/Gas 4. Place the potatoes in a saucepan and cover with water. Bring to the boil and cook for about 15–20 minutes until very soft. Drain well and return to the saucepan. Add 50g of butter and 75ml of milk and heat together gently. Mash well until smooth and creamy. Set aside.

2 Place the cod and salmon in an ovenproof dish and pour over the remaining milk. Cover with foil and cook for 10 minutes. Remove the foil and drain the milk, reserving it for the sauce.

3 For the sauce, melt the remaining butter in a saucepan and stir in the flour to make a roux. Cook for 1–2 minutes. Gradually stir in the leftover milk from the fish until the sauce has thickened. Simmer for 2–3 minutes until you have a thickened, creamy and smooth sauce. Stir in the peas, parsley and flake in the fish. Stir in the lemon juice and add the chopped hard-boiled eggs.

4 Spoon the mixture into an ovenproof dish. Top with the mashed potato and sprinkle over the grated cheese. Bake in the oven for approximately 20–30 minutes until golden and crispy. Then simply dish out and enjoy!

" As a professional rugby player, you are always looking for something which is healthy and nutritious but tasty as well (which can be very difficult). My wife came up with this recipe and, 15 years later, we are still making it and even our children enjoy it. In my eyes, you can't beat wholesome homemade food and I hope you enjoy it too. "

Martyn Williams: Cap number: 944 **Career:** 1996–2012 (100 caps)

JOHN DAWES'
PORK IN PEAR CIDER

Serves 4

700g **pork tenderloin**
2 tsp ground **ginger**
2 **fresh pears**, cored and chopped
1 x 568ml bottle **pear cider**

1 Cut the pork into 1.5cm thick rounds and place in a saucepan. Pour over enough cider to cover the meat, then sprinkle over the ground ginger and add the chopped pear. Season with a little salt and ground black pepper and leave to marinate for 30 minutes.

2 When ready, bring to a gentle simmer and cook the pork very gently for 45 minutes until it is very tender and you have a lovely reduced sauce.

3 Serve with mashed potatoes and Welsh leeks. Bon appetit!

TIP: Pork tenderloin is a very low fat meat and needs to be cooked carefully so as not to dry it out and make it tough. Slow and low temperature cooking will really tenderise the pork, leaving it soft and juicy. If you think it is cooking too quickly on the hob, simply place in a low oven at about 170C/338F/Gas 3 for up to an hour.

" When I was a student at Aberystwyth University, some fellow rugby players and I experimented in 'chef-ing'. As a result of our endeavours, we came up with this 'Pork in Cider Special'. It goes to prove all good things come from Aber Uni! **"**

John Dawes: Cap number: 694 **Career:** 1964–71 (22 caps)

JAMES HOOK'S
THAI GREEN CURRY

Serves 2

1 tbsp **vegetable oil**
3 **chicken breasts**, cut into strips
2 tbsp **Thai green curry paste**
2 tbsp **brown sugar**
Zest 1 **lime**, grated
2 sticks **lemongrass**
2 **red peppers**, halved, deseeded and finely chopped
150g **green beans**, trimmed and halved
400g can **coconut milk**
1 large handful **fresh coriander**

To serve:
150g **boiled** or **sticky rice**
Prawn crackers

1 Heat a wok and add the vegetable oil. Cook the chicken for 1 minute until golden and then add the curry paste, sugar and lime zest and cook for a few minutes.

2 Peel away the top layer of the lemongrass sticks and bash the bulbs with a rolling pin (this releases the flavour), then add to wok. Add the red peppers and green beans and toss together well.

3 Tip in the coconut milk and simmer over a gentle heat for about 25 minutes until the sauce is slightly thickened and creamy and the vegetables are tender. Add the coriander and serve with boiled or sticky rice and prawn crackers.

James Hook: Cap number: 1047 **Career:** 2006– (76 caps)

BRIAN PRICE'S
TRADITIONAL CORNISH PASTIES

Makes 6

For the pastry:
500g **strong bread flour**
120g **white shortening**
(such as lard), cut into
cubes
25g **margarine** or **butter**,
cut into cubes

5g **salt**
175ml **cold water**

For the filling:
450g good quality
braising beef
450g **potatoes**

250g **swede**
200g **onion**
50g **butter**

1 First make the pastry by placing the flour in a large bowl and adding the white shortening and margarine. Mix the fat into the flour with your fingertips until the mixture resembles fine breadcrumbs.

2 Add the water and mix in well until the mixture starts to come together to form a dough. This will take longer than normal pastry, but it gives the pastry the strength that is needed to hold the filling and retain a good shape.

3 Tip the dough out onto a lightly floured surface and knead gently to bring it all together to form a soft and elastic dough. Wrap in cling film and leave to rest for 3 hours in the refrigerator. This is a very important stage, as it is almost impossible to roll and shape the pastry when fresh.

4 Meanwhile, chop the meat, potato, swede and onion finely into 1.5cm cubes.

5 When ready to make the pasties, preheat the oven to 180C/350F/Gas 4. Cut the pastry into six equal pieces. Roll out each piece on a lightly floured surface to rounds measuring approximately 18cm. Layer the vegetables and meat in the centre of each pastry round, adding plenty of seasoning as you go. Put a knob of butter on the top of each, then bring the pastry up around the filling and crimp together to seal, or just fold over and mark with a fork.

6 Place on a baking tray and bake for 1 hour until golden, with the filling perfectly cooked and the meat tender.

" My grandfather on my mother's side is Cornish, and both my mother and her sister, John Uzzell's mother, were famous for their traditional Cornish pasties. They worked as cooks in the local colliery canteen at the Pithead Baths and all the miners loved their pasties, many of them buying them to take home. When our village, Deri, went on the annual trip to Barry Island, my mother and aunt would make up to 30 pasties for the whole family and all our friends. Either coming back from swimming or, if the tide was out, playing cricket, there was nothing better than a tasty Cornish pasty – even if it had a little sand in it! "

Brian Price: Cap number: 662 **Career:** 1961–69 (32 caps)

GERALD DAVIES'
MY MOTHER'S FAGGOTS

Makes 8 faggots

400g **lamb** or **pig's liver**
2 **onions**, finely chopped
200g **fresh white breadcrumbs**
2 tbsp **fresh sage**, finely chopped
100g **plain flour**

Ask your butcher to get hold of some pork caul for you, which is used for wrapping up these traditional faggots. Alternatively, use 8 rashers of thin cut streaky bacon.

1 Place the liver, onions and breadcrumbs in a large bowl. Add the chopped sage and season well with salt and ground black pepper. Mix well and then place in the fridge to chill and bind for about 20 minutes.

2 Preheat the oven to 200C/392F/Gas 6. With damp hands, shape the mixture into eight evenly shaped balls and sprinkle with flour. Take the pork caul and cut into pieces, then gently wrap it around the faggots. Alternatively, wrap in the bacon rashers. Place in a roasting dish and cook in the oven on a medium heat for 25 minutes until golden and cooked through.

3 Serve with boiled new potatoes, mushy peas and gravy.

Gerald Davies: Cap number: 702 **Career:** 1966–78 (46 caps)

ALEX CUTHBERT'S
CHEESY PASTA BAKE

Serves 4

400g **penne pasta**
6 rashers streaky
smoked bacon
25g **butter**
15g **plain flour**
10g **mustard powder**
400ml **whole milk**
75g **extra-mature
cheddar cheese**

1 Bring a large pan of water to the boil
and cook the pasta according to the packet
instructions. Drain and set aside.

2 Preheat the grill. Place the bacon rashers on
the grill rack and cook the bacon for about 3–4
minutes each side until golden and crispy. Pat
dry with kitchen paper.

3 In a medium saucepan, add the butter and
heat until melted. Add the flour and mustard
powder and beat until you've made a smooth
paste. Slowly add the milk a little at a time until
you have a smooth, thickened sauce. Stir in
about two thirds of the cheese.

4 Place the cooked pasta in a bowl, then
add the sauce and mix well. Crumble the
crispy bacon and stir into the pasta and sauce
(reserving a little bacon for the topping). Spoon
the pasta and sauce into a 1.5l baking dish.
Sprinkle over the remaining crumbled bacon
and grated cheese. Place under the grill and
cook for 10 minutes until the top is golden and
crusty and the filling is hot and bubbling. Serve
with a crunchy salad.

Alex Cuthbert: Cap number: 1089 **Career:** 2011– (26 caps)

GWYN JONES'
LEBANESE SALAD

Serves 4

4 large **tomatoes**, cut into 1cm cubes
1 **cucumber**, cut into 1cm cubes
6–8 **spring onions**, chopped
2 cloves **garlic**, crushed
100g **feta cheese**, crumbled
2 **pitta breads**, toasted and cut into 1cm pieces
Juice 1 large **lemon**
3 tbsp **extra virgin olive oil**
1 large bunch **flat leaf parsley**, finely chopped
1 large bunch **mint**, finely chopped

1 Preheat the grill to high. Split open the pitta breads and lay flat on the griddle pan. Drizzle with a little of the extra virgin olive oil and toast for a few minutes until golden and crunchy. Remove from the grill and leave to cool. Break into large pieces (should be quite crispy) and place in a large serving bowl.

2 Place the rest of the ingredients in the large serving bowl and toss together gently. Season with salt and ground black pepper to taste.

TIP: This is a great dish served simply on its own or, alternatively, alongisde Moroccan spiced roast lamb or griddled chilli and lemon rubbed chicken. It's also perfect served with a side dish of houmous, thick Greek yoghurt and a teaspoon of harissa paste for an added kick.

" Let's face it, rugby players like their hearty meals, which is fine when we're still playing. The trouble comes when we've retired. We think we can eat the same meals and get surprised when the middle-aged spread appears as if by magic. My biggest challenge in fighting the expanding waistline was how to make salad appealing. It was tough, but eventually I found this brilliant recipe. It takes a lot of chopping, so you can practice your knife skills – but it needs no cooking. The key is to cut everything into 1cm cubes, so that you get a bit of everything in each bite. It's fresh, it tastes great and it's really healthy. So enjoy ... you'll never think of salad in the same way again! "

Gwyn Jones: Cap number: 936 **Career:** 1995-97 (13 caps)

EDDIE BUTLER'S
VEGETARIAN BUT NAUGHTY RISOTTO

Serves 2 people with proper appetites and a love of stirring

1 large knob **butter**
1 tbsp **olive oil**
1 large **onion**, chopped
1 clove **garlic**, finely chopped
250g **risotto rice**
1l **vegetable stock**
Juice ½ **lemon**
1 big splash **dry white wine**
40g **mature cheddar cheese**, coarsely grated
40g **parmesan cheese**, coarsely grated

1 Heat the butter and oil in a large, heavy-based saucepan. Add the onion and cook for about 5 minutes until the onion begins to soften, then stir in the garlic and cook for a further minute.

2 Add the rice, stir into the onion and toss well until the rice is glistening. Lower the heat to medium and ladle in the hot stock a little at a time. Stir continuously and wait until the liquid has been absorbed before adding another ladleful. Season with ground black pepper and add the lemon juice and the wine. Don't be afraid to leave some stock unused if the rice is ready; it should be creamy, but with just a hint of bite. The whole process should take about 20–25 minutes.

3 Here you can add … well, anything. My favourite additions are, in no particular order but with a soft spot for the last: 1 large grated, boiled beetroot; 12 asparagus tips (steamed, with a squeeze of lemon juice); and 12 mushrooms (any type except button), chopped and cooked in a pan with butter and white wine.

Put any/all of these in before adding the cheese. Remove the pan from the heat and stir the cheese gently into the risotto. This looks like a lot of cheese – and it is – but the cheddar adds to the creaminess and the parmesan is simply a must. Put a lid over the pan and leave for a couple of minutes. Pour a glass of wine and enjoy the aromas. Stir one last time and serve.

> " I had two senior clubs: Pontypool and the Industrial Engineers of Madrid (Castille Regional Division 3). The Pooler played on faggots and peas, while in Spain we ate paella by the hundredweight. Only a Spaniard can cook a good paella, and I suppose the risotto is an adaptation for my limited cooking skills. "

Eddie Butler: Cap number: 784 **Career:** 1980–84 (16 caps)

RICHARD HIBBARD'S
SPICY VEGGIE BURGERS

Makes 4

400g can **mixed beans** in water, drained
4 **spring onions**, finely chopped
1 tbsp **smoked paprika**
1 tbsp **sundried tomato paste**
1 **red chilli**, chopped
1 handful **flat leaf parsley**
100g **fresh breadcrumbs**
75g **extra-mature cheddar cheese**, grated

2 medium **eggs**
1 tbsp **olive oil**

To serve:
4 **wholemeal buns**
1 large **tomato**, thinly chopped
1 **cucumber**, thinly chopped
2 tbsp **mayonnaise**
1 handful **fresh rocket**
Tomato relish

1 Place the mixed beans, spring onions, paprika, sundried tomato paste, red chilli and parsley in a food processor and blitz for a few seconds until you have a finely chopped, coarse, paste-like texture.

2 Tip into a bowl and add 80g of the breadcrumbs, the cheese and one of the eggs and mix together well, seasoning with a little salt and ground black pepper. Place the mixture in the fridge for about 30 minutes to bind together.

3 With damp hands, shape the mixture into 4 burgers. Place the remaining breadcrumbs in a shallow bowl and the egg in another shallow bowl, then lightly beat the egg. Dip the burgers in the egg and then coat in breadcrumbs.

4 Heat the oil in a large, non-stick frying pan and gently cook the burgers over a medium heat until golden and crunchy on the outside (approximately 4 minutes each side).

5 To serve, cut each bun in half and spread a little mayonnaise on the base, then top with chopped tomato and cucumber. Add the burger, some rocket leaves and a dollop of tomato relish.

Richard Hibbard: Cap number: 1048 **Career:** 2006– (31 caps)

DAVID PICKERING'S
STUFFED CHICKEN
with sundried tomatoes, goat's cheese and red peppers

Serves 4

For the stuffed chicken:
4 **chicken breasts**
125g **soft goat's cheese**
8 **sundried tomatoes**, chopped
1 small handful **fresh basil**, chopped
Juice ½ **lemon**
4 slices **Parma ham**
1 tbsp **olive oil**

For the roasted red peppers:
4 **red peppers**
2 tbsp **olive oil**
1 tbsp **balsamic vinegar**
12 whole **cherry tomatoes**

For the couscous:
250g **couscous**
600ml **chicken stock**
15g **butter**
Juice ½ **lemon**
70g **fresh rocket**
3 tbsp **fresh mint**, chopped

1 Preheat the oven to 200C/390F/Gas 6. Slice the peppers in half and remove the seeds, but keep the stalk attached. Rub the peppers lightly with olive oil and place cut side up in a roasting tin. Place 3 whole cherry tomatoes inside each pepper. Season with salt and pepper and drizzle over the remaining olive oil and balsamic vinegar. Roast for 30 minutes until softened and slightly charred. Remove from the oven and set aside, as they are best served at room temperature.

2 Place the chicken breasts on a chopping board and make an incision horizontally into the breast to make a pocket. Place the goat's cheese in a bowl with the sundried tomatoes, basil and lemon juice, and season with a pinch of salt and plenty of ground black pepper.

3 Add a tablespoon of the goat's cheese filling into the pocket of the chicken. Lay the Parma ham slices on a board, then place the chicken breasts on top and carefully wrap the ham around the chicken.

4 Heat the olive oil in a frying pan and cook the chicken for about 5 minutes on each side, then transfer to a baking tray and bake in the oven for a further 10 minutes until the chicken is cooked.

5 Place the couscous in a bowl. Cover the couscous with the chicken stock, then add the butter and a pinch of sea salt. Cover with a plate or tea towel and leave for 10 minutes. Fluff up the couscous with a fork, add the lemon juice, rocket and mint and mix together.

6 Spoon the couscous onto warmed serving plates. Slice the chicken and place on top with two stuffed peppers.

" My rugby commitments have taken me all over the world for many years, and I've been fortunate to experience wonderful food and hospitality in many countries. I miss my girls very much when I'm away from home, and there is nothing I look forward to more than a big, noisy dinner with my gorgeous family. The younger girls are great little chefs and love to help Jussie prepare supper. We all sit around the kitchen island and catch up on the childrens' news. This particular recipe is something we all enjoy – it's absolutely delicious, nutritious and healthy, and brings back warm memories of happy family times. "

David Pickering: Cap number: 802 **Career:** 1983–87 (23 caps)

J.J. WILLIAMS'
PORK IN BARBECUE SAUCE

Serves 4

4 **pork chops**
2 tbsp **olive oil**
25g **butter**
1 **onion**, finely chopped
1 clove **garlic**, crushed
2 tbsp **white wine vinegar**
150ml **water**
2 tbsp **Demerara sugar**
1 tbsp **English mustard**
1 tbsp **lemon juice**
2 tbsp **Worcestershire sauce**
6 tbsp **tomato ketchup**
2 tbsp **tomato purée**

1 Season the pork chops with a pinch of salt and ground black pepper. Heat the olive oil in a large frying pan until hot and then add the pork chops (you may have to cook two at a time) and cook each side for 3 minutes until golden. Remove from the pan and set aside.

2 For the sauce, heat the butter in the frying pan you have just cooked the chops in, then add the onion and cook over a gentle heat for 5 minutes. Add the garlic and cook for 1 minute. Stir in the white wine vinegar, water, sugar, mustard, lemon juice, Worcestershire sauce, ketchup and tomato purée. Bring to a gentle simmer, stir regularly and cook for about 15 minutes until you have a thickened, glossy sauce.

3 Return the pork chops to the frying pan with the sauce and spoon over the chops to cover. Cook gently until the chops are heated through (approximately 5–8 minutes). Serve with peas and creamy mashed potatoes.

❝ When I was playing for Llanelli I used to go back to my mother-in-law's house in Carmarthen. Mary was an excellent cook and this dish was one of her favourites. She gave this recipe to my wife, Jane (it was hand written in her own recipe book), and Jane has since frequently cooked this dish, which is as good as her mother's. It reminds me so much of my very happy days down in West Wales playing for Llanelli. **❞**

J.J. Williams: Cap number: 748 **Career:** 1973–79 (30 caps)

CRAIG & GAVIN QUINNELL'S
MADORA'S (MAM'S) RISSOLES

Makes 8 rissoles

1.5kg **potatoes**, peeled and
chopped
1 **onion**, finely chopped
340g **corned beef**,
or leftover **roast beef**
(minced)
4 tbsp **fresh thyme**
250g **fresh breadcrumbs**
200g **dried breadcrumbs**
50g **plain flour**
2 large **eggs**
1l **sunflower oil** (for frying)

1 Place the potatoes in a large saucepan and bring to the boil. Cook for 15 minutes until really tender. Drain and return to the pan and mash well with the chopped onion, corned beef (or chopped leftover roast beef), fresh breadcrumbs and thyme. Leave to cool.

2 Roll into balls just smaller than the size of a tennis ball. Place the flour onto a plate, the beaten eggs in a shallow bowl, and the dried breadcrumbs in a shallow dish. Dust the rissoles in the flour, then roll in the egg mixture and, lastly, in the dried breadcrumbs.

3 Pour the sunflower oil into a medium saucepan and heat gently. To test if it is ready, drop in a piece of bread and, if it turns golden in a few seconds, the oil is ready. Lower the rissoles into the oil a few at a time, turning frequently, and cook until golden brown. Drain on kitchen towel and place in a low oven to keep warm whilst you cook the remaining rissoles.

4 Serve with a crunchy green salad and/or homemade chips.

" The rissoles were Mamgu Cefen's recipe which was handed down to Mam. Whenever there is a Quinnell gathering, the rissoles are always the first item to disappear. If ever Mam is asked to take something to a party, the rissoles go too – they have appeared all over the world and are the stuff of legend! "

Craig Quinnell: Cap number: 934 **Career:** 1995–02 (32 caps)
Gavin Quinnell: Former professional rugby player

Paul O'Keefe

Phillip Harris

PAUL O'KEEFE'S
BEEFY'S STEAK AND ALE PIE

Serves 4

450g **braising steak**, cut into large cubes
2 tsp **plain flour**
1 tbsp **olive oil**
1 **onion**, finely chopped
1 **carrot**, peeled and cut into small cubes
1 large **parsnip**, peeled and cut into small cubes

2 sticks **celery**, finely chopped
1 small handful **fresh herbs**, such as a mixture of rosemary, thyme, bay leaf and mint
500ml **Original Stout** bottle (or 500ml bottle of Brains Dark, or 440ml

of Brains Black)
400g can **chopped tomatoes**
2 tbsp **Worcestershire sauce**
500g ready-made **puff pastry**
1 large **egg**, beaten

1 To make the filling for the pie, place the beef in a large bowl and season with salt and pepper, then sprinkle with the flour and toss around until coated. Heat the olive oil in a large saucepan and fry meat for a few minutes all over until well browned. Add the onions and fry for 1 minute, then add the carrot, parsnip, celery and herbs and cook for a further 5 minutes on a medium heat before pouring in your choice of ale. Add tinned tomatoes and bring to the boil. Stir well and add the Worcestershire sauce, then cover with the lid and simmer for 2 hours on a low heat until the meat is tender. The sauce should be nice, thick and taste delicious.

2 To make the pie, preheat the oven to 190C/375F/Gas 5, then put the meat filling

into a pre-warmed pie dish. Roll out the pastry and place over your pie dish, making sure it is slightly bigger than the circumference. Brush the rim with beaten egg, then place the pastry on top using a pie crimper to secure the edges of the pastry to the dish (or squash down with a fork or your fingers). Cut away any excess pastry with a sharp knife, then lightly score the top of the pastry with a criss-cross and decorate with a rugby ball or pint glass/bottle with leftover pastry and brush with more egg.

3 Place on a baking tray and bake in the middle of the preheated oven for 45 minutes until golden and bubbling. Allow to cool for 10 minutes before you dig in! Serve with Phillip Harris' hassleback potatoes.

 I can think of nothing better after a cold, hard, wet training session than coming home to a tasty homemade steak and ale pie (with all the trimmings). Just like my mother used to make – very nostalgic for me and extremely tasty too.

Paul O'Keefe: Injured player

PHILLIP HARRIS'
HASSLEBACK POTATOES

Serves 4

1.5kg **waxy potatoes**
50g **butter**
2 tbsp **olive oil**

2 cloves **garlic**, crushed
2 tbsp **fresh parsley**,
chopped

1 Preheat the oven to 200C/356 F/Gas 6. Using a sharp knife, carefully cut the potatoes into thin slices that don't quite go through to the other side of the potato to give a hedgehog shape. Place in a roasting tin and dot with a little butter, a drizzle of olive oil and a sprinkling of chopped garlic.

2 Roast for 30–35 minutes until golden, crunchy and cooked through. Serve scattered with chopped parsley.

TIP: Can be baked scattered with grated cheddar cheese or crumbled stilton and breadcrumbs for extra crunch. Scatter over about 10 minutes before the end of cooking the potatoes to melt the cheese and toast the breadcrumbs.

Phillip Harris: Injured player

PAUL DAVIES'
MAM'S MEAT & POTATO PIE

Serves 6

450g **plain flour**
100g **margarine** or **butter**
100g **lard**
1.5kg **potatoes**
4 tbsp **milk** or **double cream**
1 large knob **butter**
1 tbsp **sunflower oil**
1 **carrot**, cut into small cubes
1 **onion**, finely chopped
340g can **corned beef**, chopped

1 Preheat the oven to 200C/392F/Gas 6. Place the flour, margarine or butter, lard, 2 tablespoons of cold water and a pinch of salt into a mixing bowl and mix together using your fingertips until it all combines and forms into a soft dough. Tip out onto a lightly floured surface and gently knead together. Cut the dough in half and roll one piece out to cover the base of a 23cm pie tin or dish. Set the other piece of pastry aside whilst you make the filling.

2 Place the potatoes into a large saucepan and cook for about 20 minutes until very soft. Drain and return to the pan and mash with milk or cream and the butter until smooth.

3 Heat the olive oil in a frying pan and cook the carrot and onion for about 7–10 minutes until golden and softened, then add to the mash with the corned beef. Mix everything together and then spoon the filling onto the pastry base.

4 Roll out the remaining pastry and use to cover the top of the pie. Seal by crimping the edges and trim away any excess pastry with a sharp knife.

5 Place in the oven for 20 minutes until golden brown. Serve hot or cold with a variety of vegetables, salad or chips.

WELSH RUGBY CHARITABLE TRUST

" This was my mother's recipe and she used to make it all the time when we were children. And even when I was married she used to make it and bring it up to my house straight from the oven, with a tea towel over it to keep it hot. Since she passed away my youngest sister has now taken on the responsibility of making it and she does exactly the same thing as my mother did, which pleases my wife, Lorraine, as she doesn't have to cook! "

Paul Davies: : Injured player

COLIN CHARVIS'
JAMAICAN JERK CHICKEN

Serves 4

For the jerk seasoning:
1 tsp ground **allspice**
1 tsp ground **cinnamon**
½ tsp **nutmeg**, freshly grated
1 tsp **dried thyme**
1 tsp **garlic powder**
1 **hot chilli**, such as a Scotch Bonnet, deseeded and finely chopped

2 tbsp **vegetable oil**
1 tbsp **butter**, melted
2 tbsp **chicken stock**
1 tbsp **tomato purée**
2 tbsp **lime juice**
1 tbsp **white wine vinegar**
1–2 tsp **muscovado sugar**
½ tsp freshly ground **black pepper**

For the chicken:
4–8 **chicken portions**, depending on size
A few **fresh coriander** sprigs to garnish

1 Put all the jerk seasoning ingredients into a large mixing bowl and mash together until thoroughly blended. Rinse the chicken and pat dry with kitchen paper. Make a few cuts across the skin of the chicken and place in a shallow dish. Spoon the jerk seasoning over the chicken and leave to marinate in the refrigerator for at least 4 hours (longer if time permits). Brush the chicken with the marinade or turn over occasionally while it marinates.

2 When the chicken has marinated, preheat the oven to 190C/375F/Gas 5. Place the chicken on a baking tray and brush with the marinade left in the dish. Cook in the oven for 25–30 minutes or until the chicken is thoroughly cooked and the juices run clear when the flesh is pierced with a sharp knife. Serve garnished with the coriander sprigs.

" The number of times I ate jerk chicken before a match was incredible. A little taste of my grandmother's cooking whilst relaxing on a Friday evening. Somehow I could never make it taste as good as hers, but I enjoyed this little taste of Jamaica nonetheless. "

Colin Charvis: Cap number: 946 **Career:** 1996–2007 (94 caps)

JOHN TAYLOR'S
SLOW-COOKED LAMB SHOULDER
with boulangère potatoes

Serves 4–6

3 medium **onions**, finely chopped
6 large **waxy potatoes** (red-skinned variety are good), very finely chopped
4 tbsp **fresh thyme**, chopped
2kg **lamb shoulder**
8 cloves **garlic**
600ml **chicken stock**

1 Preheat the oven to 130C/266F/Gas 1. Place a layer of potato slices in the bottom of a roasting tin and then top with a layer of onions. Scatter over some fresh thyme and season with a sprinkling of salt and freshly ground black pepper. Repeat these steps to add more layers until all the ingredients are used up (the more layers the better). Season as you go with salt and black pepper.

2 Cut small incisions in the lamb and stick the whole garlic cloves in the holes, pushing them into the meat to prevent burning whilst the meat cooks, then place the lamb (skin side up) on top of the potatoes, onions and thyme.

3 Pour the chicken stock over the whole dish and place in the oven for 5 hours until the potatoes are crisp on top and soft inside.

4 When cooked, remove from the oven, cover with aluminium foil and set aside to rest for 20 minutes before serving.

Recipe reproduced courtesy of Tom Kerridge

John Taylor: Cap number: 710 **Career:** 1967–73 (26 caps)

RICHARD PARKS'
WELSH ROAST LAMB
with giant Yorkshire pudding and rice and peas

Serves 6 (or 3 rugby boys)

For the lamb:
1.5kg **Welsh lamb leg**
3 cloves **garlic**, crushed
3 sprigs **rosemary**, finely chopped
2 tbsp **olive oil**
1kg **potatoes**, chopped
2 large **onions**, finely chopped
250ml **chicken stock**

For the rice and peas:
1 tbsp **olive oil**
1 large **onion**, finely chopped
3 cloves **garlic**, finely chopped
1 tsp crushed **chilli flakes**
70g **bacon**, diced
150ml **coconut milk**
300g **long grain rice**
400g can **red kidney beans**

For the giant Yorkshire pudding:
100g **plain flour**
2 large **eggs**
200ml **milk**
50ml **water**
3 tbsp **olive oil**

1 Preheat the oven to 210C/410F/Gas 7. Score 1.5cm incisions all over the lamb using a sharp knife. In a bowl, mix the crushed garlic with the rosemary, a pinch of salt, ground black pepper and a tablespoon of the olive oil to make a paste. Rub this all over the lamb, pushing into the incisions.

2 Place the potatoes and onions in a bowl and toss together well with the remaining olive oil. Place in the bottom of your roasting tin and put the lamb on top. Pour the chicken stock over the top. Place in the oven and roast for 20 minutes, then turn the temperature down to 200C/392F/Gas 6 and roast for a further 1 hour.

3 Meanwhile, for the rice and peas, heat the olive oil in a large saucepan and cook the onion and bacon for a few minutes until they begin to soften. Add the crushed garlic and chilli flakes and cook for a further 1 minute. Stir in the rice and then cover with water and the coconut milk. Cook for 15 minutes until the rice has absorbed the liquid and is light and fluffy and the grains have separated. Stir in the beans, place a lid on the pan and set aside whilst you make the Yorkshire pudding.

4 Remove the lamb from the oven and set aside, covered in foil. Turn the heat up on the oven to 210C/410F/Gas 7. Sift the flour into a bowl, then add salt, pepper and eggs and beat to combine. Mix the milk and water in a jug, then gradually add to the flour and egg mixture, stirring constantly to create a smooth and creamy batter. Leave the batter to stand for 10 minutes.

Pour the olive oil into the bottom of a 20 x 30cm baking tray. Place the tray into the hot oven and leave for 5–10 minutes, or until the fat is smoking hot. Carefully remove the baking tray from the oven. Pour the batter into the tray and carefully return to the oven to bake for 10–15 minutes or until risen and golden brown. Resist the urge to open the oven and check on the pudding for at least 10 minutes. Remove from the oven and serve with the lamb and rice and peas.

" This is my favourite meal to cook, as it's brought me so much fun and happy memories over the years. Cooking is a way to enjoy a meal and time with mates or family, so often when training – whether as a professional rugby player or now for expeditions – food is fuel eaten between sessions and is part of a controlled diet.

Whether on a Sunday with some of the boys, recuperating with battered bodies from game day, or hunkered down surviving the sub-zero temperatures in my tent on an expedition daydreaming of this Sunday dinner, it's by far my favourite meal. In fact, this was the first meal that I had when I came home from my solo and unsupported speed record in Antarctica in 2014. It combines food elements that I have been brought up with and love – from Wales, Yorkshire and the West Indies.

I have an open-plan kitchen, which means the slightly longer cooking and preparation involved brings together sharing good times and good food with the people that I care about – and a bit of delegation of veg chopping! I hope that you guys enjoy it too. "

Richard Parks: Cap number: 1001
Career: 2002–03 (4 caps)

GARETH & GLYN LLEWELLYN'S
CHAMPIONSHIP ROAST DINNER

Serves 4

2kg **beef roasting joint**
1 tbsp **English mustard**
4 small **onions**, peeled and halved
1 bulb **garlic**
2 sprigs **rosemary**
6 sprigs **fresh thyme**
1 tbsp **plain flour**
300ml **beef stock**
200ml **dark stout** or **Guinness**

For the Yorkshire puddings:
100g **plain flour**
1 pinch **salt**
2 medium **eggs**
300ml **milk**
2 tbsp **vegetable oil**

For the roast potatoes:
4 tbsp **vegetable oil**
900g **potatoes** (King Edward or Maris Piper)

1 Preheat the oven to 220C/528F/Gas 7. Weigh the joint and calculate the cooking time, allowing 15 minutes per 500g plus 15 minutes for rare, 18 minutes per 500g plus 20 minutes for medium, and 22–27 minutes per 500g plus 25 minutes for well done. Place the joint in a roasting tin (fat side up).

2 Smear the mustard over the fat and season with salt and pepper. Roast for 30 minutes, then reduce the temperature to 180C/356F/Gas 4 for the remaining calculated cooking time. Cover with foil during cooking if the surface starts to brown too quickly.

3 Baste the joint every 30 minutes using the juices released from the beef in the bottom of the tin. To test when ready, you can use a meat thermometer, which you push into the centre of the thickest part of the meat. (For rare, the meat thermometer should read 60C; for medium, it should read 70C; and for well done, 80C.)

If you don't have a meat thermometer then a metal skewer works well. Insert into the centre of the meat and leave for 30 seconds. Pull it out and place the tip on the inside of your wrist. (If cold then the meat is not yet done; if warm then it's rare; if fairly hot then it's medium; and if very hot then it's well done.)

When the roast is done, remove from the tin and place on a carving board, cover with foil and leave to rest for 20 minutes before carving.

4 To make the gravy, spoon any excess fat out of the roasting tin then place it on the hob and sprinkle over a tablespoon of plain flour and cook, stirring just for a minute. Add the beef stock and bring up to the boil, stirring and scraping all the delicious meaty residues left at the bottom of the tin. Let it bubble for a minute, then strain and serve alongside the meat. You could add a little dark stout or Guinness to the gravy to give it a rich flavour.

5 To make the roast potatoes, peel and quarter the potatoes and place in a saucepan and cover with water. Bring to the boil and cook for 6 minutes. Drain well and then return to the pan and shake gently to rough up the edges. Put the oil in a roasting tin with a little oil from the roasting joint and place in the oven to heat up. Tip the potatoes into the hot oil and toss well. Roast for 45–60 minutes or until crisp and golden.

Gareth Llewellyn: Cap number: 870 **Career:** 1989-04 (92 caps)
Glyn Llewellyn: Cap number: 881 **Career:** 1990-91 (9 caps)

6 To make the Yorkshire puddings, mix the flour in a bowl with a pinch of salt and then crack in the eggs and mix together well. Then gradually beat in the milk to give a smooth batter.

Put a little vegetable oil in the bottom of an eight-hole muffin tin and place in the hot oven. Heat for 5 minutes until smoking hot, then remove and pour the batter into each hole and bake for about 15 minutes until well risen and crispy.

7 Carve the roast beef and serve with the gravy, potatoes, Yorkshire puddings and vegetables, such as Savoy cabbage, peas and honey-glazed carrots.

SIN BIN
Puddings and Desserts

HRH THE DUKE OF CAMBRIDGE'S
CHOCOLATE BISCUIT CAKE

Serves 8

225g **McVitie's Rich Tea biscuits**
115g softened, unsalted **butter**
115g unrefined **caster sugar**
115g **dark chocolate** (minimum 53% cocoa solids), chopped
2 tbsp **warm water** (or **dark rum** if you prefer)

For the chocolate ganache:
125g **dark chocolate**, chopped
125g **whipped cream**

Equipment:
15cm metal cake ring

1 Prepare the metal cake ring by greasing with butter and lining the sides and the bottom with baking paper. Place the lined ring onto a flat tray and leave to one side until needed.

2 Break the biscuits into small pieces (around 1–2cm in size). Do not place into a food processor – the biscuits should not become crumbs.

3 Place the softened butter and the sugar into a bowl and cream together until light and fluffy.

4 Melt the chocolate either in the microwave or over a simmering saucepan of water. Once melted, pour the chocolate onto the butter and sugar and mix thoroughly. Finally, add the water or rum and then the broken biscuit pieces. Stir well to make sure that all the biscuit pieces are coated with the chocolate mix.

5 Place the mixture into the lined cake ring and carefully but firmly push it down to create an even texture. Place the cake into the fridge to chill until the chocolate becomes firm. This could take up to 30 minutes.

For the chocolate ganache:

1 To prepare the ganache for the cake covering, place the chopped chocolate into a bowl and pour the whipping cream into a saucepan. Bring the cream to a simmer and then pour over the chopped chocolate. Carefully stir until the chocolate has completely melted and the ganache is smoothly blended.

2 Remove the chocolate biscuit cake from the fridge and from the cake ring. Place onto a wire rack with a tray beneath to collect the excess ganache.

3 Carefully coat the chocolate biscuit cake with the warm ganache, making sure that all of the cake is evenly coated. Allow to set fully before moving to your service plate and decorating as desired.

TIP: His Royal Highness suggests that you may want to add extra chocolate to the recipe!

*As featured in **A Royal Cookbook: Seasonal Recipes from Buckingham Palace (2014)** by Mark Flanagan and Edward Griffiths.*

HRH The Duke of Cambridge: Patron of the Welsh Rugby Charitable Trust

GARETH THOMAS'
WHITE CHOCOLATE BERRY CHEESECAKE

Serves 8

¼ tsp **sunflower oil**
300g **white chocolate**
600g **soft cream cheese**
300ml **double cream**
50g **caster sugar**
100g **Amaretti biscuits**
5 tbsp **raspberry jam**

180g **raspberries**
200g **strawberries**
75g **blueberries**

1 Brush a 900g loaf tin with a little sunflower oil and carefully line the base and sides with cling film.

2 Break the white chocolate into a medium bowl, place over a pan of gently simmering water and allow it to melt, stirring every now and then. Alternatively, place the chocolate in a microwave-proof bowl and heat for 1 minute on high. Stir and return to the microwave for a further 30 seconds until smooth and completely melted. Set aside to cool.

3 Place the cream cheese, cream and sugar in a bowl and beat together until smooth and light using an electric whisk. Carefully stir this into the cool, melted white chocolate until well combined.

4 Place 50g of raspberries and 2 tablespoons of jam in a bowl and mix together well. Spoon half the cheese mixture into the loaf tin, then spoon

the raspberries and jam down the centre. Top with the rest of the cheese mixture, then level the top and press in the Amaretti biscuits. Cover with cling film and chill in the fridge for at least 4 hours, preferably overnight.

5 Place the remaining jam and half of the strawberries in a small saucepan and heat gently until warmed and softened. Place in a food processor and blitz until you have a thickened sauce. Pour through a fine sieve to remove the seeds.

6 Gently turn the cheesecake out onto a serving platter, carefully lifting away the tin and removing the cling film. Halve the remaining strawberries, then arrange on top of the cake with the remaining raspberries and blueberries. Pour over some of the sauce and serve the rest separately for your guests to drizzle over.

> **"** As a professional rugby player, desserts don't feature very highly on menu choices. This doesn't mean that we don't have a sweet tooth though! I was recently invited to dinner at a friend's home and this was the dessert which was served. Absolutely gorgeous, incredibly wicked and should be kept for special occasions only (otherwise you will land up the size of a bus!) Hope you decide to have a go. Go on … be naughty!! **"**

Gareth Thomas: Cap number: 924 Career: 1995-07 (100 caps)

RYAN JONES'
CHOCOLATE ROULADE

Serves 4–6

150g **plain chocolate**
5 large **eggs**, separated
150g **caster sugar**
300ml **whipping cream**
1 tsp **vanilla extract**
4 tbsp **icing sugar**

1 Preheat the oven to 200C/392F/Gas 6. Line a 30cm x 20cm Swiss roll tin with parchment paper. Break the chocolate into pieces and place in a bowl. Sit the bowl over a pan of gently simmering water and heat until the chocolate is melted. Alternatively, place the chocolate pieces in a microwave-proof bowl and heat for 1 minute on high. Stir and then return to the microwave for a further 30 seconds until smooth and melted. Set aside to cool.

2 Place the egg yolks in a large bowl with the caster sugar and beat together for about 5 minutes using an electric whisk until thick, pale and creamy. Fold the melted chocolate carefully into the thickened egg yolk and sugar mixture.

3 In another large bowl beat the egg whites until stiff. Using a large metal spoon, fold the egg whites into the chocolate mixture, being careful not to overmix, and then pour the

mixture into the prepared tin. Place in the oven and bake for 15 minutes until risen and firm to the touch.

4 Leave to cool in the tin. Lay out a sheet of baking parchment on the work surface and dust with about 2 tablespoons of icing sugar. Turn the roulade out onto the icing sugar-covered paper and then peel away the parchment paper from the roulade. Leave until completely cooled.

5 Place the cream in a bowl with the vanilla extract and remaining icing sugar and beat until thickened using an electric whisk. Spoon over the roulade, leaving about 3cm around the edge uncovered.

6 Very carefully roll up the roulade from the long side. It doesn't matter if it slightly cracks at this stage as this adds to the finished look. Cut into slices with a serrated knife.

" This dish is ever-present at any family occasion. All of our family are 'foodies' with serious sweet tooths. "

Ryan Jones: Cap number: 1029 **Career:** 2004– (75 caps)

ROBIN MCBRYDE'S
BANANA BUNS

Makes 12

225g **self-raising flour**
100g **margarine** or
softened **butter**
75g **caster sugar**
2 large **eggs**, beaten
3 medium ripe **bananas**,
mashed
1 tbsp **icing sugar**

1 Preheat the oven to 180C/356F/Gas 4. Line a twelve-hole muffin tin with paper cases.

2 Place the flour and margarine or butter in a large bowl and rub the fat into the flour until it resembles coarse breadcrumbs. Stir in the sugar and the mashed bananas. Slowly add the eggs, mixing as you go until you have a thick, sticky batter consistency.

3 Divide the mixture between the paper cases and place in the oven to bake for 15 minutes until risen, golden and firm to the touch. Leave to cool in the tin for about 5 minutes, then transfer to a wire rack to cool completely. Serve dusted with icing sugar.

" With bananas being part of the staple diet, there are always some that reach the stage where they over-ripen. When our boys were younger they would turn their noses up at these, so my wife would use them to make 'banana buns' as a tasty alternative. The only problem is that they don't last long as they're irresistible when warm, so make sure you're around when they come out of the oven. "

Robin McBryde: Cap number: 913 **Career:** 1994–05 (37 caps)

TAULUPE FALETAU'S
DOUBLE CHOCOLATE BROWNIES

Makes 12

200g unsalted **butter**
200g **plain chocolate**,
broken into pieces
100g **plain flour**
50g **cocoa powder**
4 large **eggs**
300g **caster sugar**
50g **white chocolate**,
chopped
50g **milk chocolate**,
chopped

1 Preheat the oven to 180C/356F/Gas 4. Line the base of a 25cm square cake tin with parchment paper.

2 Chop the butter into cubes and place in a bowl with the plain chocolate pieces. Place the bowl over a pan of gently simmering water until the butter and chocolate have melted and you have a smooth mixture. Alternatively, place in a microwave-proof bowl and heat on high for 2 minutes until melted. Leave to cool.

3 Sieve the flour and cocoa powder together.

4 Place the eggs and sugar in a bowl and beat together for a good 5 minutes with an electric whisk until you have a thick, pale mixture. Pour over the cooled chocolate mixture and gently mix together. Add the flour and cocoa powder and fold in very carefully along with the chopped white and milk chocolate pieces. Pour into the prepared tin and place in the middle of the oven and bake for 25 minutes until the top is crusty, shiny and set. Leave in the tin to cool for 5 minutes, then transfer to a cooling rack and slice into squares. Delicious served warm with vanilla ice cream.

Taulupe Faletau: Cap number: 1082 **Career:** 2011– (36 caps)

ROBERT JONES'
HAZELNUT CHOCOLATE CHEESECAKE

Serves 8

100g **hazelnuts**, chopped
250g **digestive biscuits**
75g unsalted, unsoftened
butter
500g **soft cream cheese**
60g **icing sugar**

400g jar **hazelnut chocolate spread**

1 Preheat the oven to 180C/356F/Gas 4. Line the base of a 23cm round springform cake tin with baking parchment. Put the chopped hazelnuts on a baking tray and place in the oven to toast for 5 minutes until golden. Keep an eye on them as they burn very quickly. Set aside to cool.

2 Place the digestive biscuits into a food processor, add the butter and blitz until it is a fine crumb. Add 25g of the chopped hazelnuts and blitz again.

3 Tip the biscuit mixture into the prepared cake tin and press into the base using the back of a spoon. Place in the fridge to chill.

4 Put the cream cheese and icing sugar in a large bowl and mix together well until smooth. Add the hazelnut chocolate spread and mix until combined.

5 Remove the cheesecake base from the fridge and carefully spoon the hazelnut chocolate spread mixture over the base, smoothing the top.

6 Scatter the remaining chopped hazelnuts on top to cover and place the tin in the fridge for at least 4 hours, or preferably overnight. Serve straight from the fridge for best results.

" Being a rugby player and always very careful about what I ate during my playing days, the recipe I chose – hazelnut chocolate cheesecake – is certainly a luxury and an occasional treat which you can't beat. "

Robert Jones: Cap number: 831 **Career:** 1986–95 (54 caps)

ALUN WYN JONES'
NAIN'S APPLE TART

Serves 8–10

500g ready-made **puff pastry**
8 **dessert apples**, peeled, cored and finely chopped
Juice 1 **lemon**
4 tbsp **caster sugar**
75g **butter**
4 tbsp **apricot jam**
3 tbsp **water**
1 tbsp **brandy** (optional)

1 Preheat the oven to 200C/392F/Gas 6. Cut the pastry in half and roll each half into a rectangle measuring 30cm x 15cm. Trim the edges.

2 Place both pastry rectangles onto a large baking sheet. Roll out any pastry leftovers into long strips. Brush the edges of the pastry with water. Lay the strips along each side of each rectangle. Flute the edges with a round-bladed knife to create a well.

3 Place the apple slices in a bowl and add the lemon juice and toss well. Arrange the apple slices in neat rows in the well of the pastry. Sprinkle over the caster sugar and evenly dot the butter over the apples.

4 Bake in the middle of the oven for 25–35 minutes until cooked golden and the apples are tinged brown.

5 For the glaze, place the jam and water into a small saucepan, stirring continuously until the mixture is combined. Sieve the mixture and add the tablespoon of brandy (optional). Keep warm.

6 Remove the apple tarts from the oven and cover with the glaze. Serve with your choice of custard, ice cream or cream.

" Nain's apple tart is one of her signature dishes. Being an accomplished cook, she makes all of the welsh classics and much more, but this is one of my favourites. Win, lose or draw, birthdays or Christmas, it's a treat that I enjoy hot or cold. **"**

Alun Wyn Jones: Cap number: 1046 **Career:** 2006– (80 caps)

STEPHEN JONES'
POACHED PEACHES
with raspberries and vanilla ice cream

Serves 6

6 **peaches**
500g **caster sugar**
150g **fresh raspberries**
6 scoops **vanilla ice cream**
Sprigs **mint** for garnish

1 Halve the peaches and remove the stones. Place the caster sugar in a large saucepan and pour over 500ml of water. Heat until the sugar has dissolved and then add the peach halves and simmer very gently for about 15 minutes until the peaches are very tender and the skin peels away easily.

2 Turn off the heat and leave the peaches in the poaching liquid to cool completely.

3 When cold, peel away the skin and slice the peaches into quarters. Place in serving bowls with a few tablespoons of the poaching liquid, some fresh raspberries and a few sprigs of mint to garnish. Add a scoop of vanilla ice cream and serve immediately.

Recipe reproduced with the kind permission of the Sosban restaurant, Llanelli

Stephen Jones: Cap number: 966 **Career:** 1998–11 (104 caps)

ROBERT NORSTER'S
GÂTEAU BASQUE

Serves 6

For the almond pastry:
250g **plain flour**
125g **caster sugar**
125g unsalted **butter**
25g **almond flour**
Zest 1 **lemon**
Zest ½ **orange**
1 large **egg**
½ tsp **almond extract**

For the pastry cream:
1 **vanilla pod**
500ml **whole milk**
3 large **egg yolks**
100g **caster sugar**
50g **plain flour**
1 **egg yolk**, beaten

1 First make the pastry by placing the flour, butter, almond flour and lemon and orange zest in a bowl. Mix the butter into the flour using your fingertips until the mixture looks like fine breadcrumbs. Add the egg and the almond extract and mix until it comes together to form a dough. Wrap the dough in cling film and let it rest in the fridge for about 20 minutes.

2 For the pastry cream, pour the milk into a saucepan, then split the vanilla pod lengthways and scrape out the seeds into the milk and gently bring to the boil. Place the sugar in a large bowl and whisk in the egg yolks, beating for about 4 minutes until thickened and pale. Add the flour and whisk until it has all blended in. Slowly add the hot milk to it, whisking constantly. Place the cream back on the heat

and continue whisking for at least 1 minute (to cook off the raw flour taste) and you should have a thick, smooth cream. Leave to cool.

3 Preheat the oven to 180C/356F/Gas 4. Lightly grease a 20cm cake tin. Cut the dough in half and roll out to a circle measuring about 25cm in diameter. Gently line the bottom and sides of the tin with the dough.

4 Roll out the second half of the dough to about 20cm in diameter. Carefully drape it over the cake filling and pinch together the edges of the two layers of dough to seal in the filling. Trim off any excess dough. Make a criss-cross pattern on top and brush it evenly with the egg yolk diluted in a tiny bit of water. Bake for 30 minutes until golden brown.

" Unsurprisingly, the original author of this recipe began his culinary training in the Basque region of France. It's a fascinating place, known for its beauty, gastronomy, rugby and many other proud traditions, not to mention occasional political troubles! The countryside, though, is home to a rare breed of human beings – the Basque people – who are quiet fighters dedicated to the independence of their small country, perhaps not too dissimilar in many ways to the people of Wales.

Gâteau Basque is something I first discovered on one of my many visits to the area during my rugby life and one I relish every time I return. Thankfully, over the years, and with the invaluable assistance of Mrs Norster, we have perfected the art of making a version to rival the many expert local boulangers! It's most commonly made with a vanilla pastry filling, but can also be made using fruit marmalades, such as cherry or apricot with the odd splash of rum to taste. If you do use the pastry filling, make sure you let it heat for a minute to cook off the raw flour taste. "

Robert Norster: Cap number: 799 **Career:** 1982–89 (34 caps)

GEORGE NORTH'S
CARROT CAKE

Serves 8

3 large **eggs**
175ml **sunflower oil**
200g **light muscovado sugar**
1 tsp ground **cinnamon**
275g **self-raising flour**
½ tsp **baking powder**
½ tsp **bicarbonate of soda**
60g **mixed whole nuts**,
roughly chopped, plus 2 tbsp
extra for the topping

200g **carrot**, grated
100g **dried cranberries**
300g **cream cheese**
100g **butter**, softened
50g **icing sugar**
½ tsp **vanilla extract**

1 Preheat the oven to 180C/356F/Gas 4. Lightly grease and line a 22cm round loose-bottomed cake tin with parchment paper.

2 Place the eggs, sunflower oil and sugar in a large bowl and whisk for about 3–4 minutes until you have a thick, creamy mixture.

3 Sieve the cinnamon, flour, baking powder and bicarbonate of soda over the mixture and fold in carefully along with the nuts, carrots and dried cranberries. Spoon the mixture into the prepared cake tin and bake for 45 minutes until golden and firm to the touch. Another way to test if the cake is cooked is to push a skewer into the centre of the cake – if it comes out clean then it is cooked; if it is still wet, return it

to the oven for a further 10 minutes.

4 Transfer the cake to a wire rack and leave to cool completely before covering with the cream cheese frosting.

5 To make the frosting, place the cream cheese, butter, icing sugar and vanilla extract in a bowl and beat together well, either with a wooden spoon or an electric whisk, until smooth and creamy.

6 Spread the cream cheese frosting over the top of the cooled cake and finish with the extra chopped mixed nuts scattered over the top.

George North: Cap number: 1078 **Career:** 2010– (42 caps)

RUPERT MOON'S
SCARLETS' SCARLET PAVLOVA

Serves 8–10

For the chocolate meringue base:
6 large **egg whites**
300g **caster sugar**
3 tbsp **cocoa powder**, sieved
1 tsp **white wine vinegar**
50g good quality **dark chocolate**, finely chopped

For the topping:
500ml **double cream**
500g **mixed red berries**
(strawberries, raspberries and red currants)
3 tbsp good quality **dark chocolate**, coarsely grated into curls

1 Preheat the oven to 180C/356F/Gas 4. Place a sheet of baking parchment on a large baking tray.

2 Place the egg whites in a large bowl and, using a handheld electric whisk, whisk the egg whites until they form soft peaks. Add the sugar a tablespoon at a time, making sure the sugar is mixed into the egg whites well after each addition. You will have a stiff meringue mixture when finished. Spoon the cocoa powder into a sieve and dust it over the egg whites. Using a large metal spoon, gently fold the cocoa into the meringue, along with the vinegar and chopped chocolate.

3 Spoon the meringue mixture onto the prepared baking sheet and shape into a thick round using a spatula until it measures about 23cm in diameter.

4 Place in the oven and immediately turn the oven temperature down to 150C/300F/Gas 2. Cook for around 1–1¼ hours. When ready, it should appear crisp around the edges and have a dry top. The top should be firm and the centre soft and marshmallow-like. Turn off the oven and, with the oven door slightly ajar, let the meringue disc cool completely.

5 Whisk the cream until it is thick but soft. Carefully transfer the meringue from the parchment paper using a spatula onto a serving plate and spoon the cream on top.

6 Scatter over the red berries and chocolate curls to serve.

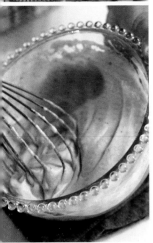

" I have such a ridiculous sweet tooth and just the thought of this recipe is making my mouth water. To play for the Scarlets and Wales was beyond my wildest dreams, but my biggest off-field ambition was to be able to cook something which looked the part. And, of course, the biggest challenge is that it had to taste the part too! This recipe is simple but amazingly effective; it has a crispy/crunchy outer and squidgy inside, just like me! I love the berries, love the chocolate and it's fairly low fat (don't count the sugar), and I now live the dream on and off the field! **"**

Rupert Moon: Cap number: 907 **Career:** 1993–95 (18 caps)

JONATHAN DAVIES'
PEANUT BUTTER CHEESECAKE

Serves 6–8

50g unsalted **butter**
200g **peanut cookies**
4 **gelatine** leaves
500g **ricotta cheese**
175g **smooth peanut butter**
175g **golden syrup**
150ml **whole milk**
300ml **soured cream**
2 tbsp **icing sugar**
80g **peanut brittle**, chopped

1 Lightly oil a 20cm round loose-bottomed cake tin and carefully line with cling film. To make the base of the cheesecake, place the butter in a small saucepan and melt. Crush the biscuits by either placing them in a plastic freezer bag and crushing using a rolling pin, or by using a food processor and pulsing until coarsely chopped. Tip the biscuits into a bowl, pour over the butter and stir until well mixed. Spoon into the base of the prepared tin and press down well with the back of a spoon. Place in the fridge to chill.

2 Place the gelatine leaves in a shallow dish and pour over water to cover, allowing them to soak for 5 minutes. Tip the ricotta into a bowl with the peanut butter and golden syrup and beat together well until smooth.

3 Place the milk in a small saucepan and heat gently. Squeeze out the water from the gelatine leaves, add to the milk and heat gently until the gelatine dissolves. Leave to cool.

4 Pour the gelatine and milk over the peanut butter mixture and mix together well. Pour onto the biscuit base, smoothing the top. Place in the fridge for about 2–3 hours to chill and firm up.

5 Put the soured cream in a bowl with the icing sugar and mix together. Spoon over the top of the peanut filling and then scatter with the chopped peanut brittle. Chill until ready to serve.

Jonathan Davies: Cap number: 1066 **Career:** 2009– (41 caps)

DAVID YOUNG'S
DAI'S DESSERT

Serves 4

4 tbsp **crème fraîche**, or **soured cream**
425g can **pineapple chunks** in natural juice
12 large **marshmallows**
200g **green grapes**, halved
4 ready-made **meringue nests**

1 Drain the can of pineapple chunks, keeping the juice in a jug for later. Place the pineapple, marshmallows and grapes in a large bowl. Add the crème fraîche or soured cream, stirring gently together. Place in the fridge until required.

2 Stir again before serving – if too thick then add a little of the pineapple juice to thin. This dessert can be served by itself, or spooned carefully on top of the meringue nests, or served with broken meringue pieces sprinkled over the mixture.

" This dessert is a reminder of memories and friendships made during my time playing rugby league. I first tasted it when new friends Mike and Sue Kuiti, who we had first met when I signed for Leeds RLFC in 1990, invited us to a BBQ. Over the coming years we became good friends and, as our families grew, we would spend most days off together.

Christmas was special to all of us, but because of playing commitments we couldn't travel home, so we would spend Christmas days together and alternate between each other's houses. Sue made this dessert as an alternative to Christmas pudding.

Since returning to play for Cardiff RFC in 1996, we have continued to make this dessert. As a family we can't eat it without reminiscing about the Kuiti family and the good times we had, and each time we serve it to our friends we tell them how we got to know about it.

It has simple ingredients and is easy to make; it is the perfect dessert for a BBQ on a hot summer's day and can be prepared in advance. You simply throw the ingredients into the bowl, chill and serve – nothing could be simpler! **"**

David Young: Cap number: 843 **Career**: 1987–2001 (51 caps)

EXTRA TIME

CLIVE ROWLANDS'
WELSH CAKES

Serves 6
Makes approximately 30–36 cakes

550g **self-raising flour**
175g **margarine**
50g **lard**
175g **caster sugar**
½ tsp **mixed spice**
125g **sultanas**
2 large **eggs**, beaten

1 Preheat a bakestone or very heavy-based frying or griddle pan. Place the flour, margarine and lard into a large mixing bowl and rub together until you have a mixture resembling coarse breadcrumbs.

2 Stir in the sugar, mixed spice and sultanas, and then add the beaten eggs and mix until you have a soft dough.

3 Tip the mixture out onto a floured work surface and, using a lightly floured rolling pin, roll out to approximately 2.5cm thick. Using a 7cm fluted pastry cutter, cut out cakes and place on the heated bakestone or heavy-based pan.

4 Cook cakes for approximately 3 minutes per side or until golden brown. Leave to cool (if you can!)

" Welsh cakes are a huge part of most Welsh families, certainly of my generation. My mother always made sure I had a tin of Welsh cakes to take with me when I returned to the RAF, or when I was in college or on away trips. They never lasted long! There are many variations of Welsh cakes, but this is my mother's recipe and a firm family favourite. **"**

Clive Rowland: Cap number: 679 **Career:** 1963–65 (14 caps)

IWAN GRIFFITHS'
DIOD FAEN (NETTLE BEER)

Serves 4

4kg **nettles** (the tips only)
5l **water**
800g **granulated sugar**
1 **lemon**, sliced
Juice 1 **lemon**
25g **brewers yeast**
1 slice **toast**

1 Pick your nettles, making sure you wear rubber gloves and cover up any bare skin. Nettles for this recipe are at their best when young in the middle of spring, just as the weather warms up, as the more established nettles are more bitter.

2 Wash the nettles, being sure to wear rubber washing-up gloves. Place in a large saucepan and cover with 2½l of water. Boil for 20 minutes.

3 Strain the liquid into an earthenware pan.

4 Place the leaves back in the pan and cover with another 2½l of water and boil again for another 20 minutes.

5 Strain into the earthenware pan. Add the sugar, sliced lemon and lemon juice to the strained liquid.

6 Place the yeast on the slice of toast and float this on top of the liquid. The yeast will react with the liquid and start to fizz, and it may look as if it is going to explode! Cover and stand until the fizzing stops, which will probably be around 24 hours but could take longer.

7 Strain, bottle and stand for a further 24 hours until the sediment has cleared. Nettle beer is best served chilled and, be warned, this can be a potent brew (see below)!

Important: This is a recipe for an alcoholic drink, so of course it's not one for children. The exact amount of alcohol is also very difficult to determine because it depends on how much sugar is in the nettles (young, spring nettles will have more sugar), so drink responsibly and you should definitely not consume before driving!

❝ This is an old family recipe and my mother remembers her grandfather making it. The first time my dad and I tried it, we corked it too firmly, too soon. The whole family was woken in the middle of the night by a series of loud bangs as the corks were shot out of the bottles and my parents were left with several dents in their kitchen ceiling! ❞

Iwan Griffiths: Injured player

ANTHONY WELSH'S
COOL CYMRU CREAM TEA

Makes 10–12 scones

For the cheese scones:
700g **self-raising flour**
3 tsp **baking powder**
4 tsp **mustard powder**
250g cold **Welsh salted butter**
3 large **free-range eggs**
250ml **whole milk**
175g **extra-mature Welsh cheddar cheese**, finely grated
2 tbsp **fresh chives**, chopped

For the tomato chutney:
1.5kg **red tomatoes**, skinned and chopped
450g **onions**, chopped
225g **brown sugar**
300ml **malt vinegar**
1 tsp **salt**

1 Preheat the oven to 220C/428F/Gas 7. Place the flour, baking powder and mustard powder into a large mixing bowl. Chop cold butter into small chunks and add to the flour. Rub into the flour until it resembles fine breadcrumbs. Add the finely grated cheese and chopped chives, reserving a little cheese to sprinkle on top of the scones.

2 Place the eggs and milk into a jug and whisk until well blended. Pour this into the mixture, keeping a little back for brushing the top of the scones, and mix and fold in until you have a soft dough. Put the dough onto a floured surface and gently press the dough with the palm of your hand until it is approximately ½in thick. Cut out scones with a 7cm cutter. Place on a greased baking tray and sprinkle with the remaining grated cheese. Cook for about 10 minutes until risen and golden brown. Transfer to a wire rack and leave to cool.

3 To make the chutney, place all the ingredients in a large saucepan and bring to the boil. Heat gently until the mixture thickens, which usually takes about 1–1½ hours. Pour into sterilised warm jars, seal and label.

4 Serve the scones with full fat cream cheese and a dollop of chutney.

“ This cream tea is a little alternative but a firm favourite with all the family; it's a real talking point and a great hit with all our visitors. It consists of homemade cheese scones, a pot of homemade tomato chutney and a pot of cream cheese (I use the best full fat cream cheese, as I find it creamier to the taste), and I use as many Welsh ingredients as possible.

The concept has been so popular that it is now one of the signature dishes at the Crumby Baker in Godalming, which is owned by our niece, Charlotte Lee. The recipes used have been passed down through my mother's family, and the scones are affectionately known as 'big granny's scones'. It can be served with an earl grey tea, a pot of coffee or a refreshing cold drink. ”

Anthony Welsh: Injured player

NIGEL OWENS'
BARA BRITH

Makes 2 x 1kg loaves

500ml **milk**
300g **caster sugar**
225g **margarine** or **butter**
500g mixed **dried fruit**
4 large **eggs**
500g **plain flour**
1 tsp **bicarbonate of soda**

1 Preheat the oven to 160C/320F/Gas 2. Grease and line the bottom of 2 x 1kg loaf tins. Place the milk, sugar, margarine or butter and dried fruit in a large saucepan and bring to a gentle boil and simmer for 5 minutes. Set aside and leave to cool.

2 When the mixture is cool, add the eggs, bicarbonate of soda and flour and mix together well. Divide the mixture between the two tins and bake in the oven for about 1 hour and 20 minutes. Leave to cool in the tins for about 10 minutes, then transfer to a wire rack to cool completely.

3 Serve cut into slices and, if you like, spread with butter.

" This recipe is a very special one for me as it is something which my late mother cooked on a regular basis. As I grew up I can always remember there being a loaf of Bara Brith in the tin. It was always freshly cooked and waiting for friends and family to share. One thing was certain, though – it never lasted long! I hope you enjoy it too. "

Nigel Owens: International referee

INDEX

The Cooks

ACKNOWLEDGEMENTS

The Welsh Rugby Union and the Welsh Rugby Charitable Trust would like to thank:

Graham and Catherine Rowlands, John and Julie Williams, David and Justine Pickering, and Warren and Trudi Gatland for allowing us the use of their kitchens. We invaded your homes but your welcome and your hospitality was second to none and truly appreciated.

Special thanks to Stephen Jones and Dwayne Peel for hosting the 'West Wales' injured players so well for their photo shoot in 'Sosban', which is their restaurant in Llanelli. Thanks also to the Vale Resort for hosting the 'South Wales' injured players' photo shoot. Your continued support is most appreciated.

A special tribute must also be paid to our injured players. You have embraced this project from the outset and have truly been a source of inspiration. We have all thoroughly enjoyed the banter, the ideas and the constant involvement. You are a wonderful group of people. Hope you enjoy your book.

Huw Evans Picture Agency, with special thanks to Chris Fairweather, for their fantastic support of this project.

Last but not least, a special thank you to our players, both past and present, for giving up their time so willingly. This book would not have been possible without your wonderful contributions and unstinting support.

Dennis Gethin
President, Welsh Rugby Union and
Chairman of the Welsh Rugby Charitable Trust